EURO NYMPHING

TIPS, TACTICS, AND TECHNIQUES

EURO NYMPHING
TIPS, TACTICS, AND TECHNIQUES

JOSH MILLER

STACKPOLE
BOOKS

Essex, Connecticut
Blue Ridge Summit, Pennsylvania

STACKPOLE BOOKS

An imprint of Globe Pequot, the trade division of The Rowman & Littlefield
Publishing Group, Inc.
4501 Forbes Blvd., Ste. 200
Lanham, MD 20706
www.rowman.com

Distributed by NATIONAL BOOK NETWORK

British Library Cataloguing in Publication Information available

Library of Congress Cataloging-in-Publication Data
Names: Miller, Josh, 1989– author.
Title: Euro nymphing tips, tactics, and techniques / Josh Miller.
Description: Essex, Connecticut : Stackpole Books, [2024] | Includes index.
  | Summary: "Author Josh Miller addresses the essentials of this
  effective method of nymphing that has become so popular around the
  country"— Provided by publisher.
Identifiers: LCCN 2023023533 | ISBN 9780811771221 (hardback) | ISBN
  9780811771238 (epub)
Subjects: LCSH: Nymph fishing.
Classification: LCC SH456.15 .M55 2024 | DDC 799.12/4—dc23/eng/20230711
LC record available at https://lccn.loc.gov/2023023533

♾️™ The paper used in this publication meets the minimum requirements of
American National Standard for Information Sciences—Permanence of Paper for
Printed Library Materials, ANSI/NISO Z39.48-1992.

CONTENTS

FOREWORD

I believe brevity is best when writing book introductions, especially fly-fishing books. It is my great pleasure to introduce you to Josh Miller—a great example of fly fishing's next generation. So let me get to the point and explain why the information in this book will help you become a better nymph fisher.

A quality instructional book is still a valuable resource for any angler seeking to improve their fly-fishing game. Instructional videos (e.g., YouTube) do provide excellent visual instruction to help any angler understand basic to intermediate fly-fishing skills. Visual learning is often the best teacher when learning any physical skill, but I believe a great book will take you deeper into the mindset of a great angler. In other words, a good book teaches you how to think like a great angler, which I believe to be the obvious progression once intermediate skills are obtained. Josh has written this book in the same manner he speaks to himself and to his students on the water to provide a next-level learning tool.

Examined experience (not just experience) is the best teacher. I've been following Josh Miller's angling career for over 10 years, and I cannot think of anyone who has logged more hours as both a fly fisher and teacher than this young man. Josh is not only a modern trout bum but a student of the game—always looking for an angle to become 1 percent better than the day before. He's a thinker and teaches his students how to think on their own. The dynamic nature of trout streams offers an infinitude of scenarios to overcome, so an angler's ability to quickly adapt to a changing environment is a must for regular success on the water.

Josh has condensed his 10,000 hours of nymphing experience within these pages, which I feel is a bargain of a lifetime. Growth is a healthy part of any successful person's life, and I can guarantee you'll grow as an angler after reading this book, as I know I will. So please let me introduce my friend and fly-fishing peer, Mr. Josh Miller. May all of you continue to seek to become better fly fishers. Good fishing!

—George Daniel

ACKNOWLEDGMENTS

Throughout my life I have been very fortunate to have had great mentors, family, and friends who have supported me in the journey. I want to take the time to recognize some of those individuals, especially ones who have looked out for me. I apologize in advance for those I might have forgotten but who had invested in me. It is important for me to recognize everyone who took time for me.

My family has been a big part of my journey and gave me the courage to write this book. I want to thank my beautiful wife, Sarah, for always loving

My wife, Sarah, and son, Jonah, fight a rainbow trout on a beautiful fall day in Pennsylvania.

and supporting me and putting up with my unstructured life. You are the best wife, and a super mother to my beautiful son, Jonah. I would not want to go through life without you.

Mom and Dad encouraged me to do the things that I loved at an early age. Dad, I will never forget the endless hours driving around in north-central Pennsylvania searching for the next trout. I now understand and appreciate all the countless hours driving, hiking, and exploring together. Even though sometimes we did not catch the biggest or most fish, it was time well spent, and never forgotten. I look forward to every trip we get to do. I hope I get to do the same with my son. Mom, you are a strong person who always looks out for others; thanks for always giving me your best. From supporting me, pushing me to be a good person, and praying for my future, thanks for being a great mom. Love you Mom, Dad, and my sister, Grace.

The first time that I can recall learning how to nymph fish was with my Uncle Donny. I will not ever forget that day with you on Toms Run in Cooks Forest, nymphing with a small white bead-head caddis larva. It is funny how sometimes you can remember something so specific: I remember exactly where I was standing, where I caught my first big trout, and even the caddis larva I was using. Those experiences are imprinted and ingrained deeply into my memory.

Joe Clark, my best friend. I am so fortunate to have a friend like you. It had to be more than just luck that brought us together. I remember the first time we met while fishing for steelhead in Erie. I hope your future is blessed and you flourish. To the many days of fishing, traveling, and car camping in Walmart parking lots! Sam Plyler, you were an inspiration and a good friend to me from the moment I met you. I am blessed to call you both friends and family.

Mark Denovich, the friend who can figure anything out. I appreciate what you have done for me and my family. Thanks for the fun times fishing, and for providing a needed home for my family during a tough time.

Bob Phillips and the International Angler crew in Pittsburgh. You all have influenced, supported, and believed in me—not only with knowledge and financial support, but with good friendships and lasting memories. Tim Lentz, for pushing me to be my best. Doug Bear, thank you for seeing something in me and pushing me to be better. You always have my back and best interests in mind, and I appreciate it.

Kalvin Kayloz, where to start? We have both experienced some crazy and fun times traveling overseas, competing and while coaching the US Youth team. How could I forget all the memorable moments, like the time you made me drive a stick shift in a foreign country for three weeks without GPS, and the time you watched as I ate tripe from a gas station somewhere near the Ukrainian border. The most memorable is the moment during a Team USA regional when the boat flipped on Lake Perez just a few minutes into the session! The times we have had, both ups and downs, are cherished memories forever.

US Youth Team wins team gold at the 20th Cortland World Youth Fly Fishing Championship in Bosnia and Herzegovina in 2023. From left to right: Tucker Horne (manager), Drew Bone (1st place Individual), Lawson Braun, Blake Hall, Noah Shapiro, Max Logan, Kage Kossler (2nd place Individual), and Josh Miller (captain). MIA BRAUN

I could not thank Sean Crocker enough for all your generosity and the time you have invested in me, especially during our times competing. Your friendship is appreciated. The entire Freestone Team—Steve Good, Kessler, Pat Weiss, Koons, Loren Williams, Anita, Bole, and my other teammates. It is immeasurable how important your influence and knowledge was for me.

John Ford, Tucker Horn, Deb Ridgway, and everyone involved with the US Youth Fly Fishing Team. Thank you for giving me the opportunity to spend so much time sharing my passion of fly fishing with the youth. It has been a great honor to help coach and mentor the team. Mike Komara, Thomas Pangburn, Holden Price, Joey Pattee, Doug Freeman, Hunter Wright, Korman Brothers, Grant Hawse, Chase Crider, Lewis Ben Comfort, Eli Buchanan, Drew Bone, Paul Bourcq, and Brian Kimmel.

Fly Fishing Team USA. It is an honor and privilege to have been a part of such a great organization. Thank you, guys, for the opportunity to fish with such incredible anglers and beautiful places. Ken Crane, Lance Egan, Devin Olsen, Pat Weiss, Cody Burgdorf, Russell Miller, and all the guys, thanks for being so generous and eager to help and share your knowledge. Jerry Arnold, and the amazing trip we got to experience together in Chile! Michael Bradley, you have been a good friend who I could always count on. Here is to the times fishing, competing, eating gas station chicken, and tying flies together in your garage!

The incredible places, experiences, and friendships that I have made throughout my fly-fishing journey are invaluable. (TOP LEFT) SAM PLYLER, (BOTTOM LEFT) CHRIS HAWTHORNE, (TOP RIGHT) JOSH MILLER

Gordon Vanderpool and Jess Westbrook, you are the best. I love the time we spend together. Gordon, thanks for the hours we shared on the water digging deep into so much technical fly fishing.

George Daniel, thanks for spending time with me, with this project, and always having my back. Hope your future fly fishing and life goals prosper. Thanks for also being a good role model for others.

Tim Cammisa, you are always there to answer my phone calls when I have stupid questions, and you give me sound advice that I appreciate. I cannot wait for you to teach me how to better fish emergers, enjoy some good pillow talk, and catch more fish than you next spring on Lake Gosling.

Fulling Mill, not because they make quality goods, but because of the faces behind the company. FM is a company run by good people. Nick Yardley, Dom,

Eric, and Chet, thanks for always supporting me and my projects and mostly for being genuine. Jesse Haller for helping me reach one of my goals. The Orvis Company, Scientific Anglers, Thomas and Thomas Fly Rods, Regal Vise, and Cortland Fly Line, for all your support.

Thanks to J Nichols for helping and guiding me through the process to achieve a lifetime goal of authoring this book. Chuck and Ben Furimsky and all my friends from the fly-tying and fishing shows.

Chris Hawthorn, I could not have accomplished writing this book without your wisdom, guidance, and support. Thank you for believing in me and taking my phone calls just to ask you the same questions repeatedly! Let's fish "Spring Crick" soon.

I also want to thank River Matt, Little Cuz, Cam Chioffi, Joe Goodspeed, Kurt Bitikofer, Jerry Armstrong, Jeff Blood, Brooks Robinson, Steve Renosky, Rodger Obley, Kris Rockwell, and Dale Fogg for persuading me to give me first fly-fishing presentation to TU in 2013.

Justin Pittman, thanks for lending me your car and being a good person, and the Precision Fly Shop crew. Torrey Collins, Joey T, and the Farmington crew. David Bower, George Costa, and the TCO crew. Jonas Price and the Feathered Hook Crew. Anyone who contributed to this book. Thank you all.

Euro nymphing is my favorite method to target trout in pocketwater. In this photo, my goal was to slow down the drift by using a high rod angle, a vertical sighter, and a single nymph. JOE CLARK

INTRODUCTION

When I first describe what euro nymphing entails to a new angler or first-timer, I start by explaining that the technique requires the angler to be centered and ultra focused. To catch the most fish, the angler must be on high alert during all aspects of the technique, implementing controlled and deliberate movements while focusing on every drift. Find the process, or the way the fish want the fly, by sampling with varied techniques like sighter angles and the speed of drift.

Euro nymphing to me is extremely visual and instinctual. If you cannot see what is going on, it is going to be difficult to catch fish. While some anglers and techniques rely on feel, I rely on sight and the environment while drifting my nymphs. Various levels of intensity and focus while fishing can correlate to how productive the angler is during their session. Sometimes when I am fishing, I often catch my focus wandering from the sighter and end up missing fish or not even noticing potential takes.

Anglers go fishing with me for various reasons. Usually I am sought out to help anglers polish or learn new types of techniques. Some anglers contact me hoping to learn methods to catch more trout. Catching more trout can be as simple as just seeing more bites. I remember one of the US Youth team members asking me how to catch 50 fish in a day. After pondering that question for a while, my response was simple: "You have to first see 50 bites before you can catch 50 trout."

Now, after many years teaching euro nymphing techniques, I have found that the hardest part for most anglers is to wrap their heads around how many bites are possible, and how many fish they are really

I intently focus on the sighter while drifting upstream in this section of stream. The bites are soft and very quick on this fishing day. Sometimes fishing requires a higher level of attention and concentration. RODGER OBLEY

missing. Euro nymphing–style techniques offer the ability to see more bites and to understand more about trout behavior. It can be one of the closest techniques to a fish's feeding habits. Once again, it takes a high amount of focus and concentration to see every bite. To learn more, an angler must be humble and admit when they missed a ton of fish. I even miss a humiliating amount of takes.

Within the semi-broad term of euro nymphing, there are many more nuances, different spins, methods, and cool techniques than just casting a weighted fly into the water. I had an older student who has been fishing for 40-plus years recently fish a day with me and say, "This technique is not the same as the high-sticking that I've done for years."

I have been lucky enough to have fished and spent time learning from some of the top euro nymph anglers in the world. Every time I fished with a high-level angler, there was always something new to learn. Sometimes I was shown a new spin on the technique, or an innovative approach or mindset. Sometimes the biggest secret can be something so small that the common angler will miss it because it seems so insignificant.

Fishing with weighted flies and a good leader can be all it takes for an angler to go from catching minimal fish to having some semi-regular productivity while euro nymphing. However, to catch even more fish, it takes time and experience to learn the depths of the technique. It also takes humility and the proper mindset.

I have always found it intriguing that a fishing style and who the angler learned from can be passed down from angler to angler, similar to painting, music, or other skills that are shared. One should always have a mentor while learning. The best parts about the euro nymphing technique, along with its incredible productivity, are the many ways, styles, and methods that all produce fish.

For instance, while fishing and competing with Team USA, Pat Weiss would often fish a session and win while using different flies and techniques (but still under the umbrella of a euro nymphing technique) than me or my teammates. This solidified for me that there are many methods to euro nymphing to catch fish. Not one way is the only way, and there is so much to learn from one another. I took those opportunities to learn as much as I could from those anglers. Instead of trying to fish like them, however, I tried to make it work for my style, developing my own instincts and way of fishing.

My intention for writing this book is to share a glimpse into my world of fishing. I like to think that there are aspects of my style, technique, and mindset

Team USA world member Pat Weiss, while fishing upstream, floats the front half of his sighter waiting for the next fish. He intensely watches for any movement or deviation in the sighter that could indicate a take. Pat is a master at making fine adjustments and detecting subtle bites with his leader system. JOSH MILLER

My learning path took many years of practicing, failing, and sometimes catching a good one. Endless opportunities are obtainable if you keep an open mind and always seek to grow. It took me around a decade of fly fishing to finally catch large wild brown trout.
ROCH MILLER

that are unique and could help someone catch more fish. My life has been surrounded by trout since I was a kid. When I think back on my childhood, I have bright memories of my mother and father taking me trout fishing in the mountains.

During my early years I used other methods of fishing. But I became increasingly determined to catch more trout, and it was not long before I unknowingly was partially euro nymphing. Using a sighter in my leader, my catch rate immediately skyrocketed. I knew I was onto something. It fueled my desire to fish in more places and spend more time on the water.

For more than a decade, developing my skills and nurturing my continual obsession with fishing, I learned the deeper aspects of euro nymphing. I was invited to help at a Team USA regional qualifier competition in central Pennsylvania. I distinctly remember judging the first session, watching every little move the angler made while fishing within the parameters of their beat. Each angler was assigned a beat, which in this case is a designated section 200 yards long.

I was intrigued by the potential to learn from talented anglers. It felt like it was the chance of a lifetime. These anglers were different. I could feel there was a lot of brain power, analysis, and strategy going into breaking apart their water.

Every beat had its own challenges, and the fishing varied greatly. They had to figure out a way to catch fish in every situation. They did not have the freedom to walk to the next beat or spot on the river; they were stuck in their section. They needed to win to earn a spot on Team USA and potentially compete in a world championship.

I took what I learned and practiced for two years then entered my first regional competition. I took silver out of 36 anglers and knew this was for me. I loved the competitive aspect because it pushed me to be my best. It also made me think and fish differently than ever before. I was subsequently recognized by Team Freestone, who wanted me to be a part of their team.

This was a dream come true because the team consisted of some of the top anglers in the northeast region—Loren Williams, Pat Weiss, Sean Crocker, Ken Crane, and many others.

After having some fun and learning so much from my team, I decided it was time to try to earn a spot on Team USA. I achieved my goal, having two top finishes at regional qualifiers and a top finish at Nationals in Lake Placid. I now had a spot on the team. I learned an incredible amount from the guys on the team, and I am so grateful for the opportunity. In addition, the guys on the team were humble enough to invite the winners from multiple world championships to teach individually at our own private clinics. At the same time, I was asked to start instructing with the US Youth Fly Fishing Team. I have been a coach and instructor for around seven years now. The time I

Head coach of the US Youth Fly Fishing Team Kalvin Kayloz and myself after a second-place finish in the world championship in the Czech Republic. KATY KOMARA

have spent teaching and learning from the coaches, anglers, and instructors is more valuable than I could ever have imagined.

I was also lucky to be spending time with like-minded anglers from different countries. Now learning from the best, I was fortunate to spend weeks at a time practicing on foreign waters in countries like the Czech Republic, Poland, Slovenia, Slovakia, Iceland, Chile, and more. I assisted Kalvin Kayloz, the head coach of the US Youth team, in three world championships. Those were some of the best moments of my life, spending time with the youth and coming home with medals.

I have been blessed to have gained knowledge that I feel would be impossible to have learned any other way. I hope to share in this book some clear and detailed tips, tactics, and techniques to help you catch more fish.

Nymph fishing has been around for a long time, and subsurface methods to catch trout are nothing new to fly anglers. However, there are some advances in techniques and technology as well as mindset that offer an innovative approach and different thought process when targeting trout.

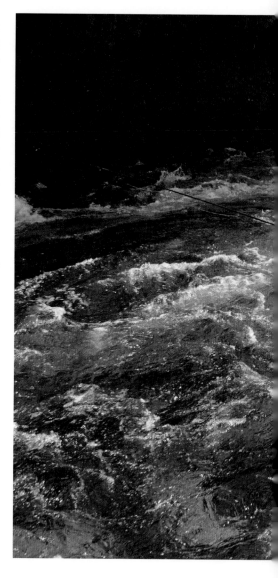

Euro nymphing is a method fly anglers use to catch trout subsurface. To best fish this technique requires the use of longer fly rods and weighted flies. Although euro nymphing can be done with gear most anglers already use, some of the gear is specifically designed to make euro nymphing more effective. The technique can be simple yet diverse, but there is more to it than just flinging weighted flies into the water.

Euro nymphing can be an everyday trout catching technique, or a method that partners with traditional fly fishing. Not only can euro nymphing help improve catch rate, but this technique will help anglers understand drifts. It also helps anglers understand more about what the flies are doing under the

Czech Republic world team member David Chlumsky systematically fishes a nice stretch of water on the river Pliva while practicing for the world championship in Bosnia. David collects important data from practice that will help him devise a plan of approach and what flies he will start with and rotate through during competition. MARTIN MUSIL

water and trout habits. The technique opens the potential to catch fish in more conditions and water types.

I remember reading about one river that sounded very intriguing to me. Upon arrival, my father quickly scoffed as we peered over the guardrail. There seemed to be an endless amount of whitewater flowing through a narrow canyon. I remember him distinctly saying, "We are fishing that? It is way too fast."

Long story short, it is now one of his favorite rivers. The drift boats quickly pass through the roughest water, with the anglers securely locked in their seats, then eventually slow down to resume fishing in the softer spots and pools. The fish occupying the quick water receive little pressure and can sometimes be exceptionally large. I would wade through the pockets to where the drift boats neglected to dissect the endless number of seams, cuts, and slots where big hungry trout could be waiting to eat a Walt's Worm.

Euro nymphing is quickly becoming a standard here in the United States. During the time I spent working in the fly shop over the last decade, I noticed the slow growth in interest in euro nymphing. Just recently it has seemed to really explode in popularity. There is one simple reason: It works, and you catch more fish! It truly is an effective method to fish subsurface for trout and grayling. Growing up, I was taught to fish with 9-foot 5-weight fly rods.

Nymphing is generally the most effective method to catch trout. Euro nymph–style fishing gives the angler an intimate approach to being in control of the flies and drifts. Seasoned anglers sometimes are hesitant to try euro nymphing, as they feel it is like indicator fishing. I can promise that it is different.

Fishing was my favorite thing to do growing up. We would use split shot and small bead-head flies. It was productive—at least we thought it was at the time—until I learned how many and how fast fish can be caught with the euro nymphing technique. I remember the first time that I used a tungsten fly without any split shot. The fly sank to depth quickly and I was connected. The bites became much more obvious and helped increase my reaction time. Best of all, there were fewer tangles.

Confidence goes a long way in fly fishing. You fish better, lose fewer fish, figure out the drifts more quickly, develop your instincts, and hopefully stick to just a few patterns. Using a simple approach and having confidence not only in your flies but in all the aspects of fly fishing will help you catch more fish.

Here are some keys to success. A good and accurate cast is the starting foundation of a drift. Carry a simple fly selection tied in various weights. Learn how to stay in better contact with your flies and how to slow down the drift. Get the flies down without hitting the bottom—my confidence is fishing the lightest flies possible—reading the sighter and detecting bites.

Anglers fly-fish for many different reasons: some to see new waters, some to learn a new technique, some simply just because they enjoy it. No reason is better than another to each individual angler. Personally, I prefer a simple approach to fly fishing, with the majority of my trout fishing done subsurface. European nymphing is a productive way to fly-fish for trout subsurface.

Euro nymphing offers a way to strategically and systematically fish. A good strategy is to grid and dissect the water to look for potential spots. A seam could be a spot where fast water is interrupted by an obstacle that slows it down. When water is broken up, fish can make even the smallest micro seams home. Once

Above: My son, Jonah, and I focused on the drift. SARAH MILLER

Left: Spending time and sharing my passion of fly fishing with family and friends is something that I love. Here my mom enjoys catching and releasing this rainbow trout. JOSH MILLER

anglers start to see the smaller seams and accurately cast to make the correct presentation, the result can be more fish caught.

We will talk about drift and drift speed a lot in this book. Simply put, drift is the way the fly moves the entire time it is in the water. Drift speed is how slow or fast we can control the fly's speed. Oftentimes my goal is to get the fly to slow down as much as it will naturally without sticking to the bottom. It can teach you how slow the water subsurface often can be. Hopefully you will eventually learn to develop your instinct and know what to do in more situations. A slower drift allows fish to see the flies longer. I try to explain to my students that the longer you can slow down, the more the fish will be tempted to bite. At times it can be impossible to drift a nymph in every spot and depression on the bottom, especially on streams with varied rocky bottoms. Slowing down the nymph over the top of the target area can encourage the fish to come up and eat the presentation. Fish rising up to eat the nymph, then moving back downward to their spot, can make the bite more obvious. Weight is often added to help slow down the drift, but with euro nymphing we have the ability to slow down the drift by manipulating our rod angles. I like to keep most of my flies simple, with more of an emphasis on controlling the drift and understanding where fish are feeding. My fly boxes are filled with fairly simple fly patterns that I have gained much confidence in.

Sometimes to catch a trout, all it might take is to slow down the presentation. Weight, body position, fly entry, and rod angles are some of the ways we can adjust our approach to help slow down the drift to entice a fish to take. AUSTIN DANDO

Joe Clark and Jerry Armstrong are aware of how spooky trout can be in low, clear water. Keeping a distance from the water, they walk the bank upstream trying to spot the large brown trout that are oftentimes sitting in skinny water on this fishery. Their approach will be floating the sighter technique with a single nymph on a long and lightweight leader.

What is possible? My friend Mark told me something a while ago that made a lot of sense to me. He said, "I thought I was doing well until I saw how many fish you can catch." Measuring success is a gray and touchy subject, but if you are reading this book you probably want to catch more fish. Having a point of reference and goals to what is possible always challenges an angler to be more productive.

Certain points may be emphasized repeatedly here to show the importance of adapting to changing conditions and situations you might encounter. I hope this book shares some simple aspects, more in-depth elements, and some deep and thought-provoking ideas to help you while on the water.

Euro nymphing can be an effective and versatile method to catch trout. The technique makes it possible to adjust the approach to fish various water types without always needing to change the setup. SARAH MILLER

1

What Is Euro Nymphing?

Euro nymphing is known around the world. It is a somewhat broad term used to describe a modern and progressive technique in fly fishing. This technique has taken many forms because in some ways it is simple and effective, making it grow quickly in popularity. Practice and fluency with this technique not only progresses the sport but also unlocks a greater understanding of trout behavior.

Some of the gear, setups, and approaches will look a bit different from what some anglers are used to. The leader sometimes is long and limited in tapers, and usually is held above the water's surface. It can be fished from loose to tight in tension, with the tippet and fly drifting under the water's surface.

Euro nymphing is a visual technique. Since focus and eyesight are important, a newer material has been introduced to fly fishing, called sighter. It is made from a colored monofilament line that helps detect bites. It will also help anglers understand how their flies are drifting through the current with more detail.

When you have a slightly loose leader connected with the flies, from the rod tip, it helps reveal a strike. The tightening or stopping of the leader and sighter helps us to more quickly detect a take. Subtle bites become more difficult to perceive and involve many hours of practice on the stream while having positive results. Bites could even be happening if the sighter slows down, stops, or deviates. In some cases, there is no indication in the sighter at all.

When introducing someone to euro nymphing for the first time, I like to convey the important lesson of seeing and counting the bites they miss. Your average angler, including myself, misses more fish than they realize. More often than admitted, fish are caught by accident. One goal as we begin euro nymphing is to try to see and register every single subtle trout bite. Speed and discernment of when to set the hook is key and comes with time and practice.

In describing euro nymphing, it is important to also understand a common truth in fly fishing. Most have heard the saying before: "presentation over pattern." My primary focus is not necessarily the fly I choose to use, but how it is presented.

The greatest asset to euro nymphing is not only detecting the bite, but also the ability to instinctively make appropriate adjustments as we are fishing. The use of a longer rod, the angles of the drift, and the

US Women's Fly Fishing Team member Tess Weigand puts in time practicing for the world championship in Norway. Tess is highly focused on each drift to not miss a fish. She strategically and thoroughly fishes the edges of a highly trafficked area on a premier Pennsylvania trout stream before working toward the middle.

Euro nymphing technique can give anglers a new outlook on water they have been fishing for years with traditional gear. David Bower practices new tricks on familiar water to slow down the drift or change the way the fly moves through the water with adjustments to his rod angles.

approach are valuable tools for changing or correcting the presentation of a fly. Bugs are not the only thing to end up in a trout's mouth. Small bits of drifting debris, with the possibility of being food, often end up in the mouth of a trout. Sometimes in a split second it is the trout that determines if it is food or not.

The casting and drifts we make with euro nymphing resemble long paint strokes. The fly and tippet placed upstream represent a single bristle on a paintbrush. The fly rod controls the stroke or drift like the handle of the brush. In the same way we paint with the direction of the wood grain, our drifts are led with the direction of the water current. The end of each drift is finished with a swift, precise hook set that accomplishes two key things. Setting the hook finishes the paint stroke cleanly and also sets us up for our next cast.

Euro nymphing reveals a new perspective for anglers. It unlocks a deeper understanding of how fish behave, how and where they eat, and what kind of presentation they prefer. It puts the emphasis on allowing the fish to dictate our adjustments. The angler has more control of the technique used in more situations. The other day, I was fishing a single 2.4 mm fly in pocketwater. I was identifying the bite and was continually late on my hook set. After missing two dozen bites very quickly, I switched to a single 2.8 mm fly. My conversion ratio from identifying bite to fish captured was instantly doubled.

Many fly fishers love to catch trout on a dry fly, including myself. But some fisheries have limited opportunities for productive dry-fly fishing. Fish are more regularly eating nymphs and other underwater food than taking flies on the surface. I often hear that trout eat upward of 80 percent of their meals subsurface. I would bet that most trout eat 99 percent of their food this way. For this reason, I have dedicated much of my time to learning the methods of nymph fishing.

I quickly learned that using weighted flies was super effective for nymph fishing. Weighted flies help us stay in contact as we cast and make drifts. The lack of external weight, like split shot, helps detect strikes even faster. Anglers need to fine-tune their weight to current conditions while fishing. We can achieve this by having flies available in different weights. Our fly boxes should consist of an organized assortment of flies tied in different weights. Organization makes changing weight a simple and smooth process.

I used to only use shorter fly rods when fishing smaller streams. But longer rods and euro tactics can be useful in some scenarios when fishing in these smaller streams. Long rods could be the ticket to reach a spot that is tough to get to or over multiple rocks and seams. Overhead cast might be impossible, but a bow and arrow cast could help place a fly into small areas. Here I use an upstream approach and a bow and arrow cast to get my flies into small areas. JOE CLARK

Fly Fishing Team USA member Devin Olsen fooled this heavy rainbow with a small nymph in fast water. DEVIN OLSEN

2

Gear

Every angler, regardless of the style of fishing, needs the right gear—and euro nymphing is no exception. The technique is becoming increasingly popular, and there is more demand for specialized equipment. Some fishing companies have noticed and started creating gear specifically designed for this technique. When I first dabbled in euro nymphing, it was difficult to find related gear, even something as simple as sighter material.

Because the popularity of this type of fishing is growing, many companies are manufacturing rods and gear specifically for this style of nymph fishing. A couple of years ago, while working in a local fly shop in Pittsburgh, euro nymphing fly rods were the number one seller.

As the technique continues to progress, the gear evolves as well; for example, now you can buy better-designed rods. Companies are recognizing that there is a market for these products and are reaching out to avid anglers for feedback and ideas as they develop rods and new gear.

An angler's setup needs to have a fly reel that helps balance out a longer fly rod; otherwise, the angler will be fighting the rod tip, making it harder to produce a smooth, controlled drift. A well-balanced setup with the correctly weighted reel balanced on a fly rod will also prevent anglers from becoming fatigued as quickly. A balanced setup makes for a more enjoyable day.

Gear like polarized sunglasses, competition fly lines, and other essentials to go into your fishing pack round out a good setup. There are always new gadgets and tools that help anglers be more efficient on the water. However, more gear is not always better. I like to limit my gear, know how to use what I have, and stay organized. In this chapter, we'll cover some gear that will help you be more productive on the water while euro nymph fishing.

EURO NYMPHING FLY RODS

Euro fly rods are longer and lighter in rod weight than regular nymphing fly rods. Having a rod designed specifically for euro nymphing will elevate your experience. There are many types and styles available.

The average length of a euro fly rod is between 10 and 11 feet long. The extra length of a euro rod helps with line and drift control. Control is important because the success of the technique depends on the angler's ability to manipulate the drift. The rod is an extension of the arm. The longer the rod (within reason), the more the angler can manipulate the flies and leader, resulting in better control over the drift. Longer fly rods also have a deeper bend, which helps maintain constant pressure while the angler fights a fish.

I was pumped when I got my first 10-foot nymphing rod—I drove the three-hour trip to central Pennsylvania. Before that day, I definitely questioned how much of a difference a longer rod would make compared to the 9-foot 5-weight I was currently using for nymph fishing. It only took a few casts to realize how much better it was. Since that day, I have not nymph fished with a rod shorter than 10 feet. I also learned how valuable a 10-foot rod is for other techniques, like dry-fly fishing.

There are many benefits to using a rod specifically designed for euro nymphing. While practicing for the world championship in Italy, the US Youth team stacks their rods of choice into the back of a rental car. DREW BONE

My first impression was how light the 10-foot rod felt in my hand. It was not too clunky and heavy as I had imagined. In the store it seemed a little bit tip heavy, but after adding a fly reel it balanced out nicely. Some anglers shy away from longer rods because it can be difficult maneuvering through the woods. The benefits of a longer rod can outweigh some of the frustrations.

The learning curve to stay out of the trees did take some time to figure out. Keeping the casts low and slowing down on my hook sets and rod movements were things that helped me stay out of the trees. Now even when fishing on small streams, I will still grab a 10-foot rod.

Length

I have noticed that anglers who have been fishing a long time are most hesitant to using longer rods. Nymph fishing relies on making good drifts. The drift is how the flies travel through the water. A longer rod helps hold line off the water at farther distances, which gives us more control over the drift and slack. The extra length of the rod will also help us fish slightly farther, spooking fewer fish.

Compared to shorter traditional fly rods, longer fly rods help anglers stay in connection with their flies longer. Connection equals bite detection, which is especially important while euro nymphing. It also allows anglers to fish over various currents, seams, and obstacles. In some situations, the goal may be direct connection between the fly rod and where the flies enter the water.

Longer fly rods pick up the line faster, like when setting a hook. They act as a bigger lever and will amplify movements as you fish. For example, a longer rod will move a greater amount of leader or fly line while mending. It will also pick up line faster when you see a strike. This will result in quicker connection to the fish. On the negative side, a longer rod has the potential to move too far, breaking off a fish during a hook set.

So, longer fly rods are better, right? Then why not use 12-plus-foot-long rods? There is a limit to how long a fly rod can be before it is harder to use. For me, rods that are much over 11 feet are more difficult to use. It can be a strain on an angler's shoulder. My shoulder has seen better days. It has been overused from prior years of not using proper technique. I would hold the rod too high above the shoulder to try to get the farthest maximum distance. It put unnecessary stress on my body. We all want to get a farther drift and catch the next fish, but it is not worth injuring your shoulder.

A world-class angler once shared with me the importance of using good posture while fishing. He said to keep my elbow bent and tucked near my body. This position will help reduce shoulder injury, he said. Anytime you have your arm straight out and your elbow above your shoulder, you are at greater risk for hurting something. Often I drive past the river and see anglers reaching as far as possible. The arm position puts extra strain on your shoulder, making you tire more quickly. Having the right length rod can help eliminate the need to hold

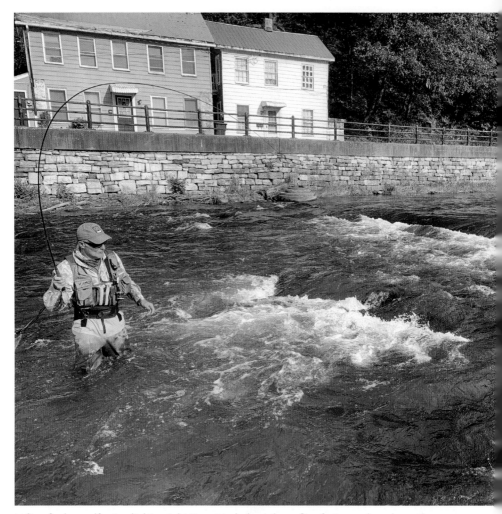

I often find myself using lightweight tippet to help sink my flies faster or slow down the drift. Rods that bend deep and leaders that stretch can help protect thin, lightweight tippet. Jeff Robinson uses a fly rod over 10 feet long that bends deeply into the rod blank, giving him the ability to use thinner tippet.

the arm so high. Elevation of the rod tip is important during some drifts, but you should also learn to use your wrist instead of extending your arm. Proper technique with the right rod will help anglers enjoy a longer day without getting fatigued as quickly.

Weight

Euro nymphing rods come in various weights and actions. When we talk about weight, we do not mean the physical weight of the rod, but the rod's resistance as it bends. I grew up using a 5-weight fly rod while targeting trout. I

was taught that was the best size to use for nymph fishing here in Pennsylvania. Sometimes I still get strange looks from anglers who are new to euro nymphing when I say that we use 2- and 3-weight fly rods. A common perception is that traditional, shorter, lighter rods do not have enough strength to land large fish. Although this can be true, luckily euro rods were designed with more backbone, giving them better ability to handle larger fish.

Euro-style rods are not your average lightweight trout rods; they are designed a bit differently from the tip to butt section. The tip section is soft, but the rear end is substantial, sometimes even more like a 5- or 6-weight. Although each manufacturer has its own formula when creating these rods, there are certain things I look for when choosing my next rod. I particularly like a lightweight rod over 10 feet that recovers quickly after a cast.

US Youth world angler Mike Komara fishes with his arm low and elbow bent, with good posture and always focusing on the target. His posture and arm position allow him to be recoiled and ready to react quickly to a take. Keeping your arm close and low will also help reduce fatigue and shoulder injury.

Fly Fishing Team USA member Michael Bradley is exceptionally good at landing large fish in a hurry with lightweight fly rods. Mike understands his gear and knows exactly how much pressure he can exert on his rod for the tippet size he is using to minimize fight time on fish.

JIMMY BRADLEY

Fly rods labeled as 2-weight vary in weight action and feel different from one company to the next. Rods can range from feeling slow and soft to fast and crisp.

The butt section starts at the rearmost point of the fly rod near the fly reel. This is where the rod gets its power. Rods with a stiffer rear section are referred to as having more backbone. If I am targeting larger fish, I grab a rod with more backbone. These rods help land the fish faster, reducing the fight time and thus causing the fish less stress before releasing them safely. This type of rod helps anglers to cast bigger or bulkier flies, make deep-water hook sets, especially important with large-profile flies, cope with wind, and better control larger fish in heavier current. I prefer a rod that has balance between a soft tip and a stiff bottom section.

Recovery is how quickly the rod goes back to its resting state. A fly rod that vibrates excessively during casting can make it less accurate, especially when using light leaders. The rod should come back into its natural position quickly after casting. If it keeps bouncing after the cast is finished, it will also cause the sighter to bounce during the drift. A bouncing sighter makes it difficult to see bites. We want smooth and controlled sighter movements during a drift. This is especially important when fish eat the fly during the initial part of the drift. We call this a reaction strike—and it is crucial to be able to detect those immediate takes.

Having a flexible and soft tip section of a fly rod is vital to euro nymphing properly, because it allows the angler to fish with light leaders and flies. A rod lacking a soft tip, like a shorter 9-foot 5-weight, is much harder to cast. The tip section of a traditional fly rod is usually stiffer, which makes it more difficult to load and cast a thin, light leader.

Although my first rod was 10 feet, it was also a 4-weight. That rod was great as I learned how to drift nymphs. It worked fine for every style of euro drift. Luckily, I have been able to try many different rods designed by various companies to see what I like best in a rod.

I switched to a 3-weight fly rod that was slightly softer, lighter, and less clumsy. It was a joy to nymph with. The rod was slightly thinner and had a softer tip section. It would bend deeper into the rear section, helping it protect thinner-diameter tippet. The longer rod became an even better shock absorber and improved my approach by protecting the light tippet.

Euro rods continue to evolve to better improve technique. Recently some have switched guide positions on the fly rod blank. Guides on a fly rod are the small loops that hold the line and leader to the fly rod. Some nymphing rods have the guide positioned far up the blank from the fly reel. The farther distance from the reel to the first guide naturally causes the line to sag. I would find myself having a tough time managing the sag. It was satisfying to test our fly rod prototypes, and help advise on small details and adjustments. Most people, when looking at a fly rod, might not think about something seemingly insignificant like guide placement, but it can be important.

Euro-type rods average between 10 and 11 feet in length and from 2- to 4-weight. ROGER OBLEY

Following are some of the attributes and ideas I consider when it is time to buy my next euro-style fly rod. I like to pick a rod that has a light action and is also light feeling in my hand. I want the rod to bend deep but recover quickly. I look for good overall balance and a rod over 10 feet. I want the rod to feel smooth and crisp.

Here is a breakdown in the weight of euro nymphing fly rods.

2-weight—The Finesse Rod

The 2-weight is my favorite size fly rod for euro nymphing. It's my go-to choice for late springtime here in Pennsylvania when trout are spread throughout shallow riffles and pocketwater. This rod size is key when anglers are targeting fish that are easily spooked and find themselves relying on thin-diameter tippet. It excels when fishing a single 2.8 mm fly in shallow pocketwater.

A 2-weight fly rod features an extra-soft tip and midsection. It helps save the angler from breaking off fish, as it will act like a rubber band, keeping fish pinned to the hook. Because the rod is softer and has a slower action, it is best matched with fishing shallower water and smaller-profile flies. The softer rod will slightly lack in power, which can be noticeable when fishing deeper water with bigger-profile flies; the slower action can cause a delay in the hook set.

For skinny water, smaller fish, small flies, and light tippet, I like the option of a 2-weight.

3-weight—The All Rounder

The 3-weight is probably the rod size that I fish most often. Even though I love the 2-weight, sometimes the 3-weight just fits the situation better. A 3-weight

Rods created for euro nymphing can also be good for other techniques, such as dry-fly, wet-fly, and indicator nymphing. MIKE KOMARA rod could possibly be the most popular option and arguably the best all-around euro rod. This size usually has a nice balance with a soft tip and plenty of power to turn fish in heavy current. A beefier rear taper will help turn over bulkier flies and assist with a faster deep-water hook set. It is great for a single- or double-nymph setup.

4-weight—The Big Water Rod

The 4-weight option is about the heaviest weight I will use while euro nymph-ing for trout. A heavier action from the rear to the tip section makes it ideal for fishing large-profile flies, and its quick action makes for a faster hook set. Extra power from this rod will help when casting through the wind. This size fly rod works well when fishing the technique we call "floating the sighter," using a heavier leader and light flies. The rod is also a decent size to carry when the angler might want to add movement to the flies by jigging or using streamers. If there is a chance to catch fish on the surface, paired with a quick switch to traditional fly line from a reel in my backpack, I will grab the 4-weight.

NOT JUST A EURO ROD

Just because it is a 10-foot rod and called a euro fly rod does not mean its only purpose is euro nymphing. Euro rods are great tools that can be used for other styles of fly fishing, like dry-fly fishing. The way euro rods are designed can benefit anglers using more traditional techniques. The extra length of the rods can help the angler get better drifts by increasing control, managing line, and fighting fish.

Fishing with an indicator setup paired with a traditional fly line (weight-forward) would have some of the same benefits when using a longer rod. The longer rod will help manipulate the fly line and stay in greater connection with

Quick Reference

- **2-weight**—My go-to size. Great for average-size trout, and the lighter action is gentle on the angler's arm and shoulder. Protects tippet in thinner diameters. Best with shallower water and lighter flies.
- **3-weight**—Great place to start. Can handle most trout sizes. Stiff enough to fish larger flies in deep water. Best all around.
- **4-weight**—Good for deep nymphing and larger flies. Handles big trout. Good for indicator nymphing. Swings wet flies and fishes dry flies well. Streamers.
- **10-foot**—Good place to start. Best in normal-size streams.
- **10-foot, 6-inch**—My go-to size. Gives an angler a slightly farther reach.
- **11-foot**—Good for large rivers. Extra reach.

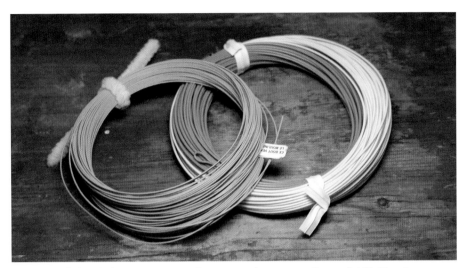

Using thin fly line helps minimize sag that causes drag on our flies and drift. Here is an example of a thin Scientific Angler competition nymph fly line next to a traditional 4-weight weight-forward fly line.

the setup. The long rod also helps with control and hook sets. Anglers who are transitioning from indicator nymphing to euro nymphing would benefit from upgrading to a longer 10-foot rod.

EURO NYMPHING FLY LINES

Although spooled on my reels, I eliminated the use of fly line for most situations and replaced it with an extra-long leader. But there are times and reasons, such as local laws, conditions, and preferences, to use fly line. In those cases, I would suggest a thin euro nymphing fly line.

Euro fly line is a bit different from a traditional fly line in a few ways. The lines are much thinner and lighter, whereas traditional lines are thicker and heavier. Euro lines can assist in some casting, but are more often used to help anglers manage line and abide by leader restrictions. While euro nymphing, it is beneficial to use the lightest and most sensitive gear possible.

When anglers choose to use a short leader with a standard fly line, a heavily weighted line like a weight-forward line will sag if it is outside the fly reel. The sag will create unwanted tension on the leader and flies, causing drag. While trying to control a drift with light flies, the weight of the heavy line will pull the leader backward as it droops between the fly rod guides. The sag is especially bad between the fly reel and the first guide, which is one reason I like a rod with a closer first guide. When a heavy fly line is outside the rod, it will pull the flies back toward the fly rod tip. These are good reasons why a thinner fly line, like a euro line, is a better choice. Less weight and sag help relieve the tension on the flies, letting them drift more naturally in the current.

Author and Pennsylvania fishing guide Domenick Swentosky is focused while fishing during a frigid winter day. JOSH DARLING

During a guide trip, I remember a student calling my setup "air fishing." He was referring to my euro nymphing setup that he was fishing with. He said it was so lightweight and sensitive that it was much more pleasant to use compared to his heavier nymphing setup.

I often use a thin leader that can be hard to grab, and especially slippery with cold or wet hands. If I find my angler having trouble finding or feeling the leader, I will cut back the leader and use a thin euro fly or thicker handling section of leader. This makes it easier to grab and feel to control slack and drift, especially on frigid days. A benefit of the euro line's thickness is that it gives an angler something to easily grab to manage slack without adding much drag to the flies.

During my time competing, there were a few rules I needed to follow regarding leaders and their lengths. The longest the leader could be was double the

length of the fly rod. There are also some places that have similar regulations, limiting the maximum length of leaders to 18 feet for use on that waterway. Make sure you always know the regulations on the waters you plan to fish.

Without getting too much deeper into fly line construction, euro nymphing fly lines are available in a few tapers. Just like traditional fly lines, the options are weight-forward, double taper, and level—sometimes referred to as a running line. The most popular type of line is the level option. My preference is a thin line that measures around .022 in diameter and has zero or little taper. The further you progress your skills, the more you will find reasons and preferences to use different options.

A thin, slightly weighted fly line like a double taper or weight-forward does have some benefits. Though not my recommendation for a first euro fly line, it can be used with techniques like floating the sighter, or help with distance on a windy day. Floating the sighter can be done with a tapered fly line to help cast a little farther with lighter flies. During windy days, having a fly line with some weight could be just the trick to help turn the day around.

The internal core (the inside of the fly line) is also important. The lines come in two styles: mono and braid core. The core gives the line its strength and a connection point to the leader. Braid core fly lines are more sensitive and supple than mono core lines. Cold water and air cause any fly line to hold coils. The braid is more supple, making it the better option in cold temperatures. Braid is also the more sensitive option, giving the angler slightly more feel while fishing. When connecting the braided fly line to the leader, options are loop to loop, nail knot, or superglue method. The right leader to fly line connection is important and will save time and frustration so you do not lose the fish of a lifetime.

Mono core lines are slightly stiffer than braid core lines. A good reason to use the mono line is the connection between the line and the leader. I like to use a blood knot to connect the butt section to my fly line if the diameter of the leader is around 8 pounds or greater. This will create a slim and smooth connection that will hold well and slide through the guides easily while fishing. A tippet ring can be added to the end of the fly line for connecting leaders that are 8 pounds and less. Mono line will hold memory, creating coils, especially in cold months. The line will also coil from being stored tightly on a fly reel. Those coils and memory in the leader can be straightened by stretching the line out before each fishing session. The trick is to pull out a few arms' length of fly line and leader before you start fishing. Start at the sighter and hold the leader arm's length apart. With gentle pressure stretch the sighter, leader, and some fly line to help straighten out everything before you fish. It is a good habit to get into. Any coils or loops can create tangles, knots, and lack of connection.

Times when I suggest the use of euro fly lines include:
- Cold weather
- Windy days
- Trouble with dexterity
- Gloves
- Local laws
- Competitive fishing
- Personal preference

EURO NYMPHING FLY REELS

Do I really need a new reel? Probably not, but if you decide to start euro nymphing there are a few key aspects to reels to know. There are now a few dedicated euro nymphing fly reels on the market, but most fly reels will work fine. The biggest difference between a traditional reel and the newer euro-style reels is how they are designed. Also, weight and balance are important when picking out the right euro reel to match with a rod. A smooth drag system is not going to hurt either, especially when using thin diameter tippet. Traditional fly reels tend to have gaps that can pinch the line. This can be especially annoying and pronounced when using a thin leader. I call this "line jumping." It can result in a lost fish or can create a weak spot in the leader. Removing the spool of the reel to get the line back into position is the easiest way to fix line jumping. I suggest using a reel with a full cage or full frame.

Some euro reels feature a large and narrow arbor. The arbor is the area on the spool that holds the fly line and leader. Larger arbors are beneficial because the line will have larger coils from the reel. Problems are caused when smaller coils are created from micro or small-arbored reels. The coils can create more tangles and tip wrap, making fishing more difficult. Larger-diameter reels will also help pick up line faster. Line pickup is nice when you get a fish and need to quickly put it on the reel, and is especially important when fishing very thin tippet. A large and narrow spool will also help reduce line cross.

Creating a good balance with your gear is important, and attaching the reel is one of those steps. Rod companies created two ways to attach the reel to the rod. Their attachment can change where and how the setup is balanced. The first attachment method is behind the cork, and the second is the downlocking method, which secures the reel to the farthest point rearward on the fly rod.

Fly reels that feature a narrow and large arbor and are designed with a full-frame cage are good choices for euro nymphing.

This will help balance longer or tip-heavy rods, because the weight of the reel is farther back, and the downlocking option will help achieve balance without using an overweight fly reel. This method pushes the weight of the reel to the very back of the fly rod, allowing the use of a slightly lighter reel to still balance the setup.

In general, the longer the rod, the heavier the reel we will need to balance the setup. An 11-foot 3-weight fly rod might not balance out the same as a 10-foot 3-weight with the same size reel. It can get a bit overwhelming when picking the right size reel for a euro rod. We know a 5-weight fly rod is matched with a 5-weight fly reel. Euro nymphing rods are slightly different because of their extra length. Longer rods need a heavier reel to properly compensate for the extra length. A traditional 4- to 5-weight reel is around the average size to balance out most 10- to 10-foot, 6-inch fly rods. It does not matter if the rod really is a 2-, 3-, or 4-weight; they will all need around a 4- to 5-weight to balance as a starting point. An average 2-weight fly reel will not balance a 10-foot 2-weight fly rod. This is where it is confusing, because previously some reel manufacturers' numbering systems were created for rods under 10 feet. Thankfully, companies are starting to create reels specifically for euro nymphing.

Oftentimes, light tippet like 6X and 7X and smaller can help create slower drifts or allow the flies to move more freely and produce more hooked fish. A smooth drag with good adjustment is more necessary to fight fish. I have personally had times when using a reel with a faulty drag lost me fish that I still am bummed about.

ACCESSORIES

Working Fly Box/Working Box

There are two types of fly storage that I carry. I was first introduced to the idea of a working box by my friend and prior head coach of the US Youth team, Kalvin Kayloz. I met Kalvin during a Team USA regional on a limestone river in Pennsylvania. It caught my eye when he opened his magnetic pack and folded down the front revealing a piece of foam filled with little flies organized in lines inside. I saw how quickly he could open his pack to grab a new pattern and get back to fishing. He did not waste time looking into fly boxes; he would just open his pack and pluck one from the foam. After the session he took the time to show me the small foam insert in his chest pack. The insert was, in theory, his working box, and he had his flies lined up and organized by importance and in multiple weight options. In other words, he had the same fly in multiple bead sizes for different weights depending on the water depth and flows. There was also a small section of "oh crap"–conditions flies, like eggs and attractors.

That small section of oh crap flies was another lesson on its own. He had flies to help him overcome tough situations such as when conditions change, like dirty water, or if fishing is harder than anticipated. Without getting too detailed, he had San Juan worms for dirty water, a streamer or two for covering hard-to-reach places, and an egg and stonefly just in case.

It was not until I got into competitive fishing with my friends that I really started to make the most of using a working box. During practice when a fly would start to produce bites and fish, I would stop using that fly, take it off, and put it in my working box. I would then switch to a different fly pattern to see if it would continue to produce fish. If it would work and catch more fish, then it would go second in the working box. My goal was to see how many flies would catch fish during practice to give me more options while competing. My conclusion was that there were more flies that would work than I realized. It started to change my perspective that flies are the most important part to catching fish. When anglers are catching fish on a particular fly, why would they take off that fly? Fish eat more flies than I realized. I would remove a fly that was catching fish just to put on another fly and continue to catch fish. I recognized how unimportant the fly pattern is *at times* and was beginning to understand that presentation is even more important than the fly. How I was fishing the fly, with intention and confidence and making proper adjustments, took precedence over the fly pattern.

The goal was to fill the working box with multiple fly patterns that worked in practice in order to have more confident fly options while fishing during a competition session. When it came time to fish in the competition, I would already have all my fly choices in order in a small box. Here is the way I now fill up a working box with flies.

While fishing a local stream, Nick Meloy has his flies organized by weight and fly type in a working box attached to his fishing vest. A working box helps organize and simplify fly selection for quick adjustments.

The C&F chest pack is a good choice to help keep flies organized and easily accessed.
RODGER OBLEY

A working box can be anything that can hold flies, like a small fly box or a fly patch on the outside of an angler's pack or vest. The purpose is to help keep us organized and focused by limiting excessive options in flies with just a few key patterns. The working box has definitely changed my methods and mindset to fly fishing with a minimalist approach. I like to either use a small single-size fly box or work directly from a C&F fly patch attached to my fishing pack. The C&F is nice because it makes it easy for me to quickly change flies because of its convenient position on the outside of my pack.

I like to preload my working boxes with a limited number of flies that I think will be useful during the next fishing session. I try to avoid carrying too much equipment, including multiple fly boxes in my pack. Most anglers try to carry too much, making it difficult to find the right pattern, or even risking potentially losing a fly box, like I have done several times.

Prior to the fishing session, fill your working box with flies depending on where you are fishing. The point is to limit the amount of fly choices to just a few. Organize the flies in the working box in order of weight, importance, and confidence. Flies are important to catching fish, but their weight and how we drift those flies with our approach is just as important. The advantage of having a limited number of fly options in the working box is that we can convert our mindset to focusing on the drift and not relying on or blaming the fly pattern for the reason we are not catching fish.

Pro Tip

Working boxes are great for narrowing down your selection to patterns you are confident in. On the stream it is important not to second-guess yourself about fly selection. First find the right spot, then go to a small box loaded up with good options for the average angling scenario. —Cam Chioffi

I fill my working box with flies that I have found to work and put them in order of importance. I make sure I have six to a dozen of each pattern set up in order in my box. It is important to have at least a few of each pattern because it is possible to lose flies very quickly while nymph fishing. The first fly patterns I add to the box are always my confidence flies: Walt's Worm, France Fly, and Frenchie—available in multiple weight options. These flies have absolutely become my confidence patterns that I trust to help me produce fish. Organizing by weight is crucial to euro nymphing properly, so I make sure to have each pattern in multiple weight options. I first have my three confidence flies tied in an appropriate weight for the river I am fishing next.

I carry larger fly boxes filled with more fly options in my backpack or a storage fly box in the vehicle. The larger boxes are mainly used to fill my working box depending on my next fishing outing. The main point of the working box is to limit fly choices so you do not open a large box with too many options. I have found that working from one large fly box is overwhelming.

In my first national championship, I remember having a difficult session. Halfway through and with no fish, I desperately opened my fly box, revealing what seemed like an endless amount of fly options. It was slightly overwhelming being against the clock. I remember thinking, *What do I choose?* But looking back on that day, I wish I had known how to read the water better, had better connection, fished an area of my section that I ignored, or just made slower drifts. Today, limiting myself to a few fly choices in a working box compels me to rely on making good drifts and not wasting time pondering over fly selection. A good drift is just as important as the fly pattern.

Recently I fished a session on a stream in central Pennsylvania. I forgot to load my working box from the session previously, and I accidentally left my larger fly boxes at home. When at the stream I opened my working box only to find about 12 flies, and they were all Walt's Worms in the same color and size. Luckily there were at least a few different bead sizes to give me an assortment of weights. Long story short, I caught plenty of fish. It was reinforcement that drift, approach, mindset, and adjustments are so vital. I believe most fly patterns will catch fish.

These bugs were captured on a small spring creek in south-central Pennsylvania. Fly patterns like a Walt's Worm can be mistaken for scuds, shrimp, and cress bugs by a trout.

While fishing a beautiful stream, I look into my small, thin working box. I used to carry a lot of fly patterns, but now I try to only carry a box or two of flies. Having a simple fly selection helps me make a quick choice and forces me to focus on technique and my approach instead of relying on the fly pattern. DOMINIC LENTINI

Good fly boxes are waterproof and lined with quality dense foam that will securely hold heavy weighted flies. Some fly boxes offer a middle page that doubles the amount of flies the box can hold. I like to start each year with a fresh new fly box and reorganize my flies. Flies can degrade, and the hook can become weak if they sit in a box for too long.

I added a backup box because of what happened to me once during a competition. While fishing this competition in central Pennsylvania, I remember quickly crossing the stream in high water. I forgot to take the time to close my fishing pack, and my fly box with 900ish flies sank to the depths. Now I always carry a backup fly box in my backpack just in case!

Tippet

Many anglers neglect to consider the importance of tippet. Tippet is the connection between the flies and the sighter, and the last link that we rely on to keep the fish from breaking off. Tippet options mainly are available in the two types: monofilament and fluorocarbon. For euro nymphing, the average size tippet we use is between 4X and 7X. I use Fulling Mill products.

Having a good, strong tippet in thin dimensions is important, because it will be more supple and give the fly the ability to move more freely and get to depth quickly. Thinner tippet will also help slow the drift down so it will appear more natural. Slower drifts give the fish more time to see and move to the fly.

It is good to have an assortment of tippet in assorted sizes. There are times when it is beneficial to use a heavier tippet that has a thicker diameter to reduce sink rate. Thicker-diameter tippet is also important when it is necessary to quickly fight a fish so it is handled safely. It will also help anglers lose fewer flies! For most cases, your assortment of nymphing tippet should range between 4X and 7X.

Fishing Packs

During my years working at a fly shop, anglers would regularly walk in looking for their next fishing pack. I would tell them it is similar to buying a vehicle—there are so many options, and some people like trucks and others like cars. Chest packs, hip packs, slings, and vests are some of the most popular options. Some of these packs are more practical for euro-style angling, with efficiency in mind.

The top option I would recommend to customers is to purchase a chest pack. Chest packs are a good choice because they are usually comfortable, having two over-the-shoulder straps instead of a neck strap that could irritate your neck. Comfort obviously makes for a more-pleasant experience and will keep us in the game longer.

There are some chest packs that even come with a small backpack to help balance out the front of the pack nicely. A small backpack area is great to carry a few extra supplies and usually has a clever way to secure a fishing net high on your back.

Chest packs can be worn slightly higher on the body than most packs, letting anglers wade even deeper without getting the pack wet. Euro nymphing is a short-range technique, and sometimes getting close to the target is necessary. It is the only option for me because I am about 5-foot-something.

The style of a chest pack is also good for keeping gear organized and for ease of access. As a competitive angler, simple but efficient is what I am after. I am not looking to carry every fly box and little piece of gear I own, just the essentials. While fishing, it is nice to have designated spots for gear in small pockets for quick use.

Net placement is also important when thinking about purchasing your next fishing pack. I have seen nets attached in obscure ways or not attached to the angler at all. I have also seen a few nets floating down the river. I have noticed that many packs and bags seem to lack a way of attaching and securing a net. Chest packs usually have a designated way to attach a net, called a D ring. The D ring is usually located higher up on the back of the pack.

Sunglasses

Polarized glasses are essential to any type of fly fishing, including euro nymphing. Though they help us look stylish while fishing, polarized glasses have a

Even until the last light of day, I still wear my polarized sunglasses for safety and to detect bites. A low-light lens is a good option when fishing in low-light conditions like early morning or late evening. A good trick in the morning is to put them on before you start fishing to help your eyes adjust. JOE CLARK

much more important use, depending on whom you ask, of course. Polarized lenses are designed to help reduce glare and help us better see into the water. They help eliminate the shine on the surface of the water so anglers can wade safely, spot more fish, and detect more strikes.

The crazy thing is that when anglers come to me for guided trips, they commonly forget to bring sunglasses. Before my anglers arrive, I remind them that a pair of sunglasses is just as important as any essential gear. Sunglasses will protect your face and eyes from briars and sticks while trudging through the woods and are especially important when anglers are casting and flies are swinging through the air.

Some sunglasses seem to help magnify the sighter material while euro nymphing. Polarized sunglasses come in a few lens colors and tints that can be more helpful for anglers when fishing in different conditions and water types. For example, a blue lens color is great for fishing big waters like lakes and the ocean. Copper, green, and amber are also good lenses for trout fishing. Mirrored and sunglasses with dark lenses are best for super bright and sunny conditions. Yellow is good for low-light conditions like early morning, rainy days, or during the evening hatch. Euro nymphing is very visual.

Personally, I have found it important to carry two different pairs of glasses, with a dark and light lens color, for different conditions. The first pair is a Smith with an amber lens color. It is a dark lens, making it ideal for high sun conditions. The amber lens color has been great for fishing lakes and even when I fished for bonefish on the flats in the Bahamas.

Second is the pair of polarized sunglasses I use most, a Smith in a yellow lens. The yellow is perfect for low-light and overcast days, especially in the eastern United States where it is often is dreary. Sometimes the best fishing can take place early in the morning or at the end of the day when the sun is on the horizon and the lighting gets dim. The yellow lens is bright enough for those low-light times. These color sunglasses give me a longer amount of time to see while most everyone on the river has already removed their dark-lensed glasses.

Knowing that some fish species are extra active in low-light conditions, wearing a low-light lens makes sense. I remember coaching in the world youth competition in Poland a few years back. The area was beautiful, and the landscape reminded me of something I would see in central Pennsylvania, with green valleys and tree-lined rolling hills. There was also a thick cloud of fog hovering over the water, making for extra low-light conditions most of the day, but the fish did not mind. Actually, I think it even made fishing better.

Wax

Wax, also known as floatant, is another essential part of your gear. I was aware that wax was important while dry-fly fishing, but I did not realize how fundamental its use is while euro nymphing. Friend and teammate Sean Crocker was the first person to explain to me how to effectively use wax and how much it would benefit my drifts. Wax will help anglers get a better drift at a distance or can be important when floating the sighter. Now I find myself going through a good amount of wax every year.

Any euro drift can benefit from the use of wax. There are techniques during a drift that require your leader to float high on the surface of the water. Line, leader, and sighter that are not waxed will start to sink below the water's surface, making it harder to lift the line from the water. Trying to lift the line off the water during the drift could pull or lift the flies because of the tension created

Pro Tip

Using floating grease for your nymphing indicator will help you with longer-distance casting so as not to sink your indicator in the first seconds after the cast and provide you with contact with your flies all the time. —Martin Musil

Pat Weiss generously applies wax to his sighter and leader to help keep it floating high, which will assist him while mending and help him detect very subtle takes.

from the line sinking beneath the surface. The wax will keep the leader and sighter floating high above the water, making it easier to avoid pulling the flies, letting them drift more naturally.

Wax should be generously applied to the leader, fly line, and sighter with your fingers or a small application pad. Depending on my approach and technique, I will apply wax from the fly line through the leader down to the end of my sighter. The wax can even be used on the tippet to restrict the flies from sinking as quickly for times when fish are feeding high. Thicker leaders and more knots make for more surface area to hold greater amounts of floatant, which keeps the line floating longer. Thinner leaders might need wax added more regularly.

Sighter Wax

Brightly colored wax is a cool new product that can even be used on an adjustable and removable sighter. The wax can help anglers adjust their depth without needing to change tippet length. The wax also can be used to brighten up a fixed piece of sighter material that is in a leader. The sighter wax is a useful tool for quick adjustments while euro nymphing. A good option is Skafars colored wax. The wax can get a bit messy if it is too warm and is harder to use in freezing temperatures.

A few years back I was watching Roe Bear fishing during a session in a Team USA regional. He was on a beautiful section of water, one of my favorite sections. The section is so productive because the water is varied in depth—from

As a world-level competitor, Tess Weigand understands and practices the importance of making quick adjustments. She adds to the leader highly visible and removable wax that can easily be adjusted or used to help her see bites in low-light conditions.

shallow, skinny edges to deep, rocky pockets. I noticed before the session began that he was rigged with a longer section of tippet from the sighter.

He chose to start his session at the bottom of his beat. That section of water is very skinny and shallow. He opened his pack and pulled out a thin tube of bright orange sighter wax. It looked like a tube of Chapstick. He rubbed the wax onto his tippet with his thumb against the wax to create a sighter. The wax created an orange-colored sighter that was about 1 foot long and about 3 feet from his fly. Now the length between the fly and the new wax sighter was more appropriate for that shallow water.

What was most intriguing to me was how fast he adjusted as he moved upstream to deeper water. His current wax sighter now would need to

Fluorescent sighter wax can be added to an existing sighter or to add a visual section to tippet or leader.

be fished under the surface of the water to get the flies deep enough in the new section he was fishing. He grabbed his tippet, and using a rag he quickly removed the wax. Then he reapplied the wax higher up the tippet to create a new sighter about 4 to 5 feet from the fly—a perfect length to properly fish the deeper slot. Fish came to hand quickly.

The wax gives anglers the ability to adjust quickly on the go without having to change tippet length and waste time tying knots. The wax can also be applied to existing sighters to help anglers see them better. The sighter can be challenging to see when the sun is low and there are no leaves on the trees. Extra glare on the water as well as snow are also times when the sighter can get lost during a drift. The wax is brightest and easiest to see on thicker-diameter lines like monofilament. Wax is available in multiple colors. It seems to work best and stick to the line well when the wax is warm.

Nets and Retractors

Do not underestimate the importance of a good net. Nets with the proper mesh can help capture fish quickly, limiting over-fighting and exhaustion. I like to carry what most would say is an oversize trout net. Several times I have heard anglers call down the stream: "Boy, that's a big wishful-thinking net." Well, I would rather be ready for the time I hook that next mega brown trout, and I have the right size net to land it quickly and safely!

I like to have a large, hooped net with a rubber coating that will help me land and secure fish in a hurry. I was able to quickly land this brown trout after it swam downstream through fast whitewater. It would have been difficult to land it safely without a net.

A net is an essential piece of gear to safely secure fish, handle them with care, and provide a proper release. The big basket makes it possible to control the fish and never have to lift the fish from the water. I cannot count how many times my oversize net came in handy while trying to land a heavy fish in swift water. A good net should have rubber mesh. The rubber is much safer on fish than the older rope/cloth material. And we try our best to not overhandle fish by lifting them out of the water even while in the net. There is no perfect and safe solution, but having a net will ensure more safely handled and released fish.

Nets can be expensive, and that is why I recommend using a retractor. I have seen anglers try to attach their net to themselves in some obscure ways. I have also seen a number of those nets floating downstream. Securely attaching a net helps an angler be more efficient while fishing, making it faster to grab and replace the net after releasing a fish. I attach my net just below my neck in the center of my back.

I will add the retractor to the rim of the net, slightly offset, about 4 inches from the handle. Two reasons are because it lets the handle hang slightly offset so it is easier to grab, and it also helps bring the net higher up on my back. This worked exceptionally well once while walking through brush; I would just keep walking until the net would release from the thorns and retract to my back.

Joey Takeman safely secures this beautiful brown trout in his net. JOSH MILLER

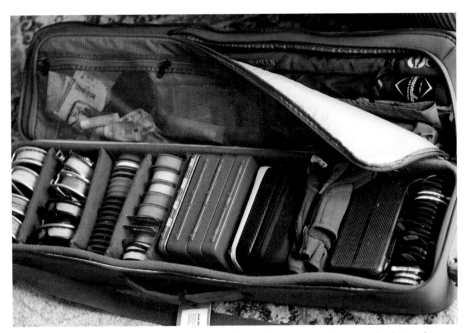

One of my favorite pieces of gear is the carryall. The Orvis Carry All is a good solution for anglers on the go and can hold lots of essential gear.

Carryall

Rods and gear are an investment. A good carryall will not only help protect your gear, but also keep it organized and easily accessible. I like to use the Orvis Carry All. It is my favorite option because of the ease of use and how much I can fit into it. This and my chest pack are my favorites. I have two of these awesome travel pieces: one for trout and the other for steelhead. It makes it easy knowing I have the right gear when I grab the right one as I walk out the door on my next trip. It is filled with essentials like extra tippet, leaders, and leader-building supplies, and a first-aid kit. I also have an extra pair of sunglasses, some accessories like Aquaseal, and a few reels just in case. The rod compartment holds a bunch of rods; I think there are about eight crammed into mine currently.

The use of a lightweight leader paired with a good cast helped me quickly gain connection with my flies. This fish, sitting in fast, shallow water, ate the flies the second they entered the water. ROCH MILLER

3

Leaders, Lines, and Knots

If you were to ask 50 of the top world euro nymph anglers about their leader formula, you might get 50 different answers. That answer could be shocking, thought provoking, or even frustrating. To me, that's proof there is more than one way to be successful. Although the leader is particularly important, I like to keep leaders on the simple side. I try not to overthink or overcomplicate leaders, but spend more time working on technique, mindset, and approach.

Two big instances stand out in my mind when I think about my evolution in euro leaders. The first one was when Pat Weiss taught me the proper knots for connecting leader materials and attaching leaders to the fly lines. The second was to rethink that I needed to use heavily tapered leaders for euro nymph fishing. It took me many years to transition from heavily tapered euro leaders to leaders built with fewer and thinner sections until it was practically level.

The leader is a connection of lines that bridges the gap between the fly line and our flies. Leaders can be designed with different lengths and different weights to help anglers fish in various water conditions. Traditional fly-fishing leaders average around 9 feet in length, but euro nymphing leaders are much longer, often exceeding 18 feet. The advantage of a longer leader is to help eliminate drag caused by the fly line on the water.

When the fly line is outside the fly rod and on the water, it has some disadvantages, like spooking fish, and it can be harder to manage and control the drift. The weight of the fly line can cause sag, creating unwanted drag on the flies. The sag can pull our flies and limit how far away we can properly nymph fish. The use of a longer leader can help anglers get a more natural drift. Leaders that are extra long can be used without any fly line at all, which is often how I fish. This helps eliminate unwanted sag and tension but can be more difficult to control and cast at first. Anglers can use an extra-long leader to eliminate fly line from ever coming from the reel. This approach can be referred to as a mono rig; long butt sections can be added to the rear of the leader. The leader's overall length can range from 30 feet to much longer. The main benefit is to get drifts without the interference of the fly line, or to effectively get drifts without needing to purchase a euro-style fly line.

Materials used to build leaders are changing and evolving. Materials like Cortland Camo, Maxima, and Pierre Sempe have been my go-to for building euro nymphing leaders. Lighter, stronger, stretchy, and more-supple materials have given me the ability to execute technical drifts and produce more fish.

Leaders can be designed with purpose, for fishing a specific way or to accomplish a specific drift. I challenge you to experiment for yourself. Everybody will eventually develop their own personal style and preference. Options in nymphing leaders can range from level (no taper design) to heavily tapered with many

A slight adjustment to the leader to help compensate for a heavy downstream breeze was the ticket for capturing this beautiful fish. Having some knowledge of leaders and how you can adjust the sections can help you overcome obstacles like wind or get the flies presented in diverse ways.

sections. I like to make sure my students have some understanding of leaders and how they work.

Lighter leaders can help you fish farther distances with less drag. However, they can be more difficult to cast at first. Heavier leaders are a little easier to cast, but will sag more, causing drag. Often sag is unwanted, as it will pull the flies and cause drag. A thin, little, or non-tapered leader sags less, giving the angler a long, uninterrupted drift. With practice, fishing a light leader can put you ahead of the pack.

Sometimes leaders will hold the shape that they came in, which is called memory. Leaders built with thicker materials with high memory can hold coils and be hard to straighten out, making fishing clumsy. That can limit the angler's distance and overall sensitivity. Lighter, more-supple leader materials will help magnify bites and make for a more sensitive setup. However, sometimes a stiffer or heavier leader is good for other casting-based techniques, like floating the sighter while fishing with lightweight flies. It is beneficial to know how to adjust a leader to overcome river conditions and properly use different techniques. Building and adjusting leaders will also help with obstacles like wind.

I recommend taking the time to learn how to build your own leader and to practice. This gives anglers the creative ability to adjust the leader for what they need to accomplish in different situations. Creating a leader is not difficult; you only need a few materials and a few types of knots to make it happen.

EURO LEADERS

A basic understanding of the different sections of a leader will help anglers know how and when to make necessary adjustments. *Not all euro leaders are the same*—an unlimited number of formulas and options exist for creating a leader. Some leaders are built for casting heavy flies, while others are designed for techniques like floating the sighter. Knowing a few basic reasons why we use different leaders for different techniques will help you pick the best ones for your situation.

I was taught that there are two mindsets when it comes to finding the right leader. One is an all-purpose leader that is more rounded for fishing multiple techniques like euro, dry dropper, and single dry fly. The other is more focused and specific, designed more on a single technique or style.

The coaches of the US Youth team would teach the importance of using an all-around leader while competing. The main reason was to be able to switch between techniques while fishing without wasting time on adjusting the leader or grabbing another fly rod. An all-around leader gave anglers the ability to not only fish nymphs but potentially fish a single dry-fly or dry-dropper setup with the same leader. The all-around leader fished everything decently, though not one technique perfectly. In competition, it is a race against time, so quick adjustments are key.

Adjustments take time but are sometimes crucial to make. Fly Fishing Team USA member Russell Miller enjoys the process and wastes no time when it comes to making necessary adjustments. JAKOB BURLESON

Although there are times when I will use leaders that are good for multiple approaches, I have found that I tend to stick to a dedicated and more specific nymphing leader. The all-purpose leader I use is created with heavier pieces tied together with multiple tapers. This makes the leader slightly heavier, making it harder to fish at a distance with light flies. I like it when I am in situations when I can use a more specific lightweight leader because that is what I enjoy most.

Building a taper in the leader *can* help cast flies more easily, especially very lightweight flies while floating the sighter. Dry-fly leaders are tapered for an important reason. The taper helps cast a fly that is wind resistant and very light-weight. However, we do not always need a tapered leader while nymphing. We can depend on weighted flies to help load the rod to make a cast.

The lack of knots in level leaders makes it simple and quick to tie even while on the water. Leaders tied with multiple knots can hang up in your guides, which could simulate a strike. It is faster and easier to build leaders with fewer sections, and it is easier to carry less leader material on the stream if you need to repair or retie a leader. By tweaking and adjusting the materials and sizes you are using while building a leader, you can adjust your approach for the stream. Sections and pieces of leader can be changed to create slack or to make it easier to fish in the wind. Knowing about leaders and how they are designed will help anglers approach the water differently.

I sometimes change sections of my leaders to overcome obstacles. For example, I might feel the need to use a heavier leader and sighter when fishing in the wind. I might switch to a thin sighter and leader if I want to be tightly connected to my flies. You can adjust the leader to present the flies in different ways.

LEADERS AND TRANSITIONS

Let us turn our focus to the rear of the leader, what we call the butt section, which is what connects to the fly line. The butt is usually the thickest section of a leader and can be different lengths and diameters. Some leaders will have a long, level butt section directly connected to the sighter, while other leaders will have many tapered sections that step down in diameter until they reach the sighter.

The sighter is the visual part of the leader that helps the angler detect bites and helps us to understand what is going on during the drift. The sighter is a crucial part of any euro leader. Sighters range from 02X to 6X with the average size around 3X. I like to build my sighter into a leader that is about 2 feet long.

Conditions create exceptions, and I try to find a balance using the thinnest sighter material you can see. Thin and supple sighter material is more sensitive to help detect bites and can be fished on a tight line at far distances. The downfall to a thin sighter is that it can be more difficult to see, and it can break more easily. Thicker-diameter sighters are usually easier to see. The problem is that

Leaders with limited or no knots slide smoothly throughout the fly rod while managing line.
DOMINIC LENTINI

heavier sighters sag more and can hurt our drift. This could be a time to use wax to brighten a thin sighter.

Thicker-diameter sighters can be helpful when anglers want to fish methods like floating the sighter. It will suspend drifts for longer and help with seeing the takes. The larger-diameter footprint of thicker sighter material lies better on the water and can help it float higher and longer. Again, depending on water conditions, we might need to adjust our approach. The thicker material also has more surface area to hold more wax to help its buoyancy. Having said that, a larger-diameter sighter material on the water's surface can spook fish, especially in clear water.

Sighter material is available in several color options. Alternating colors like orange and yellow or red and pink seem to be the most popular. The alternating colors give contrast and a point of reference that can be picked up quickly by the eye. A white sighter is good against a green and wooded background, but white will blend in with turbulent water. Yellow, green, and orange are my favorite colors and are decently visible against most backgrounds. A good option is the Cortland yellow sighter in 4X. It is very bright and holds its color well. Second is the Pierre Sempe in 4.5X. It is thin but strong and highly visible.

When creating a leader, it is important to add sizes of sections that are similar in diameter and stiffness. If you try to connect a thick line to a very thin line, there will be an abrupt and harsh transition. This will make it difficult for connection and create a potential breaking point. We want to connect lines close in size and stiffness, so the transition is smooth. Transition is how the materials transfer energy and power through to the next piece of line. If the leader is going from a stiff piece to a soft or supple piece, there can be a hinge or another potential breaking point.

One trick to help see the transitions is to use a method that my friend Joe Goodspeed showed me. Once you have made your knot, with one hand grab a piece of the leader, then in your other hand grab a second piece after the knot. The knot connection between the two sections should be in the center. Hold about 2 to 3 inches on either side. Try to create a semicircle with the knot at the top of the arc. This will show you how the materials transition between each other. Sometimes going from a stiff to a soft material will not form an even semicircle. This is an example of a connection that does not transfer energy as well.

There should also be a smooth transition between the leader and sighter. Oftentimes I see anglers with a harsh transition between their maxima to the softer, more-supple sighter. The trick to "soften" the transition is to use a small section of fluorocarbon in between the sighter and leader material. I typically add a small piece around 18 inches long that is the same diameter as the sighter. This line helps create a more gradual transition between the leader and sighter.

Materials that I currently use for building and adjusting leaders. Leaders created with stretchy material will help absorb a heavy-handed hook set to protect lighter tippet. However, when fishing larger and bulkier flies, stretch in the leader could create a delay in the hook set, resulting in a missed fish.

The softer connection makes a smooth transition that will form a more natural belly in the sighter to aid in bite detection.

Building a proper leader for euro nymphing requires having a few essential materials. There are many options, and materials to help build a euro leader are constantly evolving and changing. Here are my favorite choices.

Maxima and Cortland Camo are great materials for building a section of euro leader. Available in many sizes, the most popular for euro nymphing is from 6 pounds to 20 pounds. The material makes for a good rear section of a euro leader. Pierre Sempe is thin, but it does not compromise in strength, which makes this material an excellent choice when building lightweight euro nymphing leaders. The material is available in small diameters from 6X to 1X. Its light weight and thin diameters make it ideal for fishing at a distance with minimal drag. Pierre Sempe is a colored line, available in multiple colors. A brightly colored line is great because the entire leader will be visible to the angler.

Micro and Thin Leaders

Some of my favorite options are micro and lightweight thin leaders because lighter leaders can improve sensitivity and control and help us fish at a distance. It has advanced my approach, especially while fishing pocketwater. After the learning curve with casting, the leader can be very accurate.

Youth world angler Noah Shapiro using a lightweight leader in skinny water on a mountain stream in Italy. Noah is in control of his drift and makes every bite count as he prepares for the World Fly Fishing Championship. JOEY PATTEE

The second advantage of the lighter leader system is how fast I can make connections with the flies. I have experienced countless times when fish eat the fly the second it breaks the water's surface, referred to as reaction strikes. Connection is necessary for strike detection. Without instant connection, I would have missed or never even noticed the fast bites.

Because the leader is much lighter, traditional casting like roll and overhead casting becomes slightly more difficult. It takes time to develop accuracy while fishing this way. Learning casts like the Frisbee cast and 180 rule (see Chapter 5) will help you better and more accurately use lightweight leaders.

Keep in mind that some fishing areas have restrictions on the overall length of leader. Make sure you know the regulations on lengths before you fish! Leaders can be shortened or modified by cutting a length of material from the butt section.

Leader Formulas

Josh's Micro Leader
- 12 feet Sempe Spirit (Nylon Fluo Bicolor Orange/Jaune) in 3X
- 8 feet Sempe Spirit (Nylon Fluo Bicolor Orange/Jaune) in 4X
- 2 feet Sempe in 4.5X

Josh's Lightweight Leader
- 10 feet Cortland Camo in 8-pound
- 8 feet Cortland Camo in 6-pound
- 2 feet Fluorocarbon in 4X
- 2 feet Cortland Sighter (yellow) in 4X

All-Purpose Leader
- 6 feet Maxima Chameleon in 14-pound
- 4 feet Maxima Chameleon in 10-pound
- 2 feet Maxima Chameleon in 8-pound
- 2 feet Fluorocarbon in 3X
- 2 feet Fulling Mill Sighter in 3X

Floating the Sighter Leader
- 10 feet Maxima Chameleon in 14-pound
- 4 feet Maxima Chameleon in 12-pound
- 2 feet Amnesia as sighter (orange) in 10-pound
- 2 feet Amnesia as sighter (green) in 8-pound

Cody Burgdorff Everyday Leader
- 12 to 14 feet Copolymer in 4-pound
- 8 inches Umpqua Sighter in 4X

Mike Komara Everyday Leader
- 8 feet Maxima Chameleon in 10-pound
- 3 feet Maxima Chameleon in 8-pound
- 1.5 feet orange Siglon .008 inch
- 1.5 feet Hanak Sighter in 5-pound

Fish can sometimes be very wary, just like the rainbow trout in this spring creek. A long, light leader helped me cast accurately in between the vegetation at a slightly farther distance without causing a disturbance. ROCH MILLER

CONNECTING

Connections like knots and loops are how we attach everything together. These connections are important for creating smooth transitions for when we manage our line during a drift. Luckily, you do not need to know every knot in the handbook to be a proficient angler. I suggest learning the proper way to tie a few simple knots.

Traditionally, the most popular connection between a leader and a fly line is called loop to loop. Most manufactured fly lines come with a small, welded loop that is knotless at the end of the line. The smooth loop makes attaching a leader

Pro Tip

Level leaders are ideal much of the time due to improved sensitivity, reduced sag and wind drag, and ease of casting through the fly rod guides. —Cody Burgdorff

to the fly line quick and easy. Using thin leaders with the loop connection to the fly line seems to work fine. Loop to loop also works when connecting the light leader with a Davy; an improved clinch knot works well, too.

Attaching a heavier-diameter euro leader to the loop on the fly line would not be my desired choice. Rather, this is when a nail knot connection or a specialty fly line with a mono core would be helpful. When fly lines do not have a loop, my choice of connection is a blood knot or nail knot, depending on leader diameter and the core of the fly line. The blood knot is a good choice when using a mono core fly line; the nail knot when using a braid core fly line. Mono fly lines have a center "core" made with a mono line. Using a blood knot to attach the leader to the mono core of the fly line makes a smooth and strong connection.

The trick is to remove the coating of the fly line to expose and use the inside core. The fly line core will then be directly connected to the leader, making an almost seamless transition. This connection is best used with leader materials from 8 to 15 pounds. When removing the coating on the fly line, the goal is to expose just enough core to tie a blood knot. For me to properly tie a blood knot, I need about 3 to 6 inches of fly line. Here is how I do it.

Cut a piece of 3X tippet material about 18 inches long. Thin but strong tippet will cut through the coating of the fly line easily. Take that tippet and create a loop. Place the loop 6 inches down the fly line. Cinch the tippet loop around the fly line, allowing the tippet to slice the fly line coating down to the

A good fish is a product of properly tied knots. You do not need to know the handbook of knots to be a successful angler, just a few tied well. ZAK BART

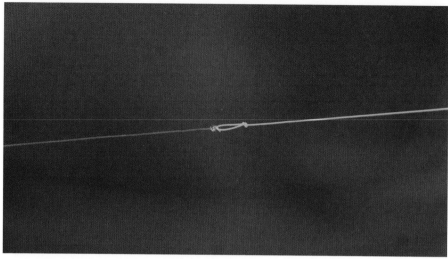

The perfection loop is a simple knot that creates the shape of a loop that helps with quick connections. I use this knot at the end of my sighter material in place of a tippet ring. Using a perfection knot or tippet ring will help keep the piece of sighter the same size while fishing.

core of the mono. Keeping pressure on the tippet with one hand and holding the fly line with the other, pull the tippet to remove the fly line coating. The coating should come off in one piece. If not, repeat the steps until the core is clean. Attach the leader directly to the fly line using a blood knot. Make sure to trim the tags of the knot close so nothing will hang up when sliding through the guides.

The blood knot was a good choice when I started to build euro nymphing leaders. I recall an evening sitting in Steve Good's basement with all my leader-building supplies covering his pool table. I was trying to assemble a new leader to use on a central Pennsylvania stream in a competition session the next day. Halfway through the process, Pat Weiss gradually slid over my shoulder to look at the connections. I remember him telling me in a subtle way that I should use another method rather than the surgeon's knot.

He recommended that I use a blood knot. He explained that the tag ends come out from the knot at a 90-degree position, making it easier to pass through the guides. The blood knot can also be used to add tippet or attach sighter material. The way the tag comes out of the knot is another good option to add dropper flies to your setup. This knot also makes it easy if you need to add or change something far back in the leader.

MULTIPLE-FLY SETUPS

While euro nymphing, anglers often fish with multiple-fly setups. When using two or more flies, we call the extra flies droppers. Dropper flies can be attached

I prefer the tag fly of a two-fly setup to be on an independent section of tippet. It seems to let the fly have more movement during the drift.

Joe Clark makes sure his flies are spaced apart at the proper distance, which is for the safety of the fish and also to drift in multiple columns of water.

in several ways, such as from the eye or the bend of the hook. I attach a dropper fly from a piece of tippet created when I tie a knot.

Tags are from a piece of scrap line cut off after tying two pieces of tippet together. Doing this will give the flies more movement while fishing. When using the tag system, the dropper flies have slightly more slack and the ability to move more freely in the water.

I love pocketwater, and I also love using a single-nymph setup. Water that is broken into many current seams by rocks and structure is a good scenario for a single-fly setup. ROCH MILLER

To attach a dropper to a tag, add 2 feet of tippet to the end of your setup using a surgeon's or blood knot. There should be two pieces of scrap line (called tag ends) protruding from the knot that normally would be cut off. Use one of the tag lines to attach the dropper fly. I keep the tags for my dropper flies on the shorter side, around 2 to 4 inches. The problem is that tag lines over 6 inches quickly tangle around the other piece of tippet. If you tie the tag line too short, it will be difficult to attach a dropper fly. Find what works for you.

ONE FLY VS. TWO

When I was developing my skills, I had a habit of always wanting to use two flies at once. I thought more flies meant a better chance to catch a fish. I soon learned that in some situations fishing a single fly on your line can be the ticket. Water type, stream conditions, and how the fish are feeding are just some criteria for determining when to fish a single fly or multiple flies on your setup. Here are some guidelines on when to use multiple flies.

Single-Fly Setup

Fishing with a single-fly setup is my confidence rig when fishing shallow pocketwater. This type of water can be turbulent, with many rocks that break up the current and create micro seams. That can make it more difficult to control and slow a multiple-fly setup. One of the flies will undoubtedly get caught in a different current or seam and affect the drift.

Fishing a single fly will cast more accurately into small targets. Sometimes the target zone might be a foot-long spot behind a rock or the bank. It would be challenging to fish accurately with a two-fly setup when the second fly is 20 inches from the first. One of those flies will not be in the zone, affecting the presentation. Using one fly will help you stay in direct connection and reduce drag. A two-fly setup can cause a slight disconnection between the point or bottom fly. A lack of connection can result in a missed or even undetected bite.

Streams with overhead structure are preferably fished with a single nymph. When you find yourself

A stream that is full of varied current speeds created by pockets and rocks is an ideal situation to euro nymph with a single fly. Alternating currents can make it difficult to control and slow down a multi-fly setup. Here I am using one 3.0 mm France Fly while fishing this beautiful stretch of stream. JOE CLARK

Here I am using a shallow-angled drift in skinny water. This is a time when I like to use a two-fly setup. The low and shallow angle created through the rod and sighter and a slight lead with the rod tip can encourage both flies to continue through the drift and not hang up on the bottom. JOE CLARK

caught in the trees, one fly has a much higher chance of dislodging than multiple flies.

Also, consider using a single-fly setup when the fishing is hot. When landing fish with two flies, the other fly often gets tangled around the fish or in the net. This can be true if the fish eats the dropper or upper fly on the line. If you are quickly catching fish, try using just one fly. It will help reduce tangles and in turn keep your flies in the water longer.

Multi-Fly Setup

One scenario when I start with a two-fly setup is when approaching a larger body of water. A uniform current that is waist deep can be difficult and sometimes intimidating to fish. In larger bodies of water, fish can be spread out and suspended throughout the column. Fishing two flies in this situation gives your approach a multi-level drift.

I will use a two-fly setup when I am prospecting to find where the fish are holding. One of my flies on the setup will be an attractor and the other a small, natural fly. In theory, the attractor is used to catch the attention of a fish. The fish might not eat the bright attractor but could eat the natural-looking second fly. This searching setup can be especially useful in cold water.

Also, a two-fly setup works well when fish are keyed into eating small bugs. Often on tailwaters and highly pressured streams, fish sometimes seem to prefer eating small bugs. A small nymph like a midge can be fished with a heavier fly to help get it to depth. The heavy fly can be used either on the tag or point position.

Pro Tip

Fish a single fly. Fishing one fly gives you a more direct connection, creates less drag on the setup, and allows for more accurate weight tuning. Most importantly, a one-fly setup tangles significantly less and is much faster to change flies. —Mike Komara

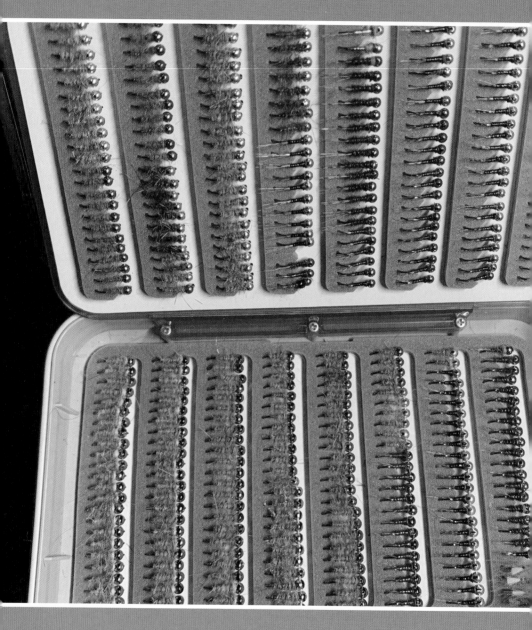

A fly box organized by fly size and weight. Previously when tying my flies, I would use a specific-colored thread to help me identify the size of the bead. Now my trick is to create a mark on the back of certain size beads with a Sharpie.

4

Flies

Some anglers put a lot of time and thought into finding the right fly patterns to fill their fly boxes. I was one of those anglers. I spent hours looking through books and searching the internet for inspiration on new fly designs to use on my next fishing outing. But through my years of fishing, travel, and experiences, I have simplified the flies that I regularly use. I like to take the approach of using nymph patterns that should work 365 days a year instead of specific patterns for a certain day, river, or hatch. A simple fly selection has helped me build confidence on any trout watershed I come across.

Of course, there are times when fish can be selective and key in on specific bugs. The problem is there are countless varieties of insects and fly patterns tied to look like specific bugs throughout their life cycle. There are honestly too many fly patterns to pick from, so how does an angler narrow down their fly choices to a few patterns that will work?

As a young angler I always imagined there were top secret patterns that only elite anglers knew about and were sworn to keep secret. I regularly stopped into the fly shop near my house as a kid to talk with local fly-fishing legend Jim Hoey. I would try to persuade him to share one of these top secret fly patterns. Every time I would ask Jim, he would not budge. It was hard to get those secrets from him!

One special day he finally decided it was time to share. I was shocked and surprised. I was disappointed that the flies he thought were top secret looked like patterns I was already fishing and were quite simple. It was the first time that I heard someone say that the secret was the *way* he was fishing those flies. In other words, it was the technique not the flies. That statement stuck with me from that day on. He also said he was confident in those flies and would fish them intentionally, knowing he would catch fish. I was not looking for that answer. I was looking for a magic pattern that would help me catch more fish! But now I get it.

The focus should not just be on finding the right pattern but on researching better or deeper techniques, mindset, or approach. A fly-based mindset can lead the angler to think the reason they are not catching fish is because of their fly, when there could be so many other reasons. These reasons can include drift, controlling speed, tension, slack, weight, and approach, which can all be improved with practice.

I think that a fly should be as natural as possible to what is normal to the fish. A fly that is reasonable size, shape, and color presented with a good drift will catch fish in most situations. In this next section, I will discuss things that are important, things that can matter, and things that can be situational.

EURO FLIES

There are flies tied to look very realistic; they can look similar or be mistaken for the actual bug. Euro nymph–style flies are simpler flies tied to replicate a broad spectrum of bugs. The biggest difference is that euro flies rely on weight to help them sink to the appropriate depth, where the fish are feeding.

A suggestive pattern like the France Fly looks close to the real thing.

I spotted this fish from the bank and took my time as I moved into a close position. On my first cast I quickly saw that my Walt's Worm was too light, as it swept downstream much quicker than I wanted. I made a quick switch to a Walt's Worm that was one size heavier. As the fly sank on the first cast, the fish was easily fooled by the plain and simple Walt's Worm.
ROCH MILLER

The weight added to the fly generally comes from tungsten beads in varied sizes and colors. The euro nymph flies that I like to fish are on the smaller side, with an emphasis on their shape. The size ranges from #16 to #20. How the fly is designed can dictate how fast or slow the fly sinks. Its shape, profile, and size will help either slow down or speed up how fast it sinks to the bottom.

Euro nymph–style flies are an essential part of fishing this way. A fast descent will lengthen our time in the zone where fish could be feeding. Weight that is built directly into the flies will help us stay in connection. Euro nymph flies will also give anglers the option to fish more water types, like skinny, shallow water or fast water. Weight is easily adjusted by changing the actual fly or can be adjusted by using a smaller or larger bead. I always carry the same fly patterns in an assortment of bead sizes to offer more weight adjustments while fishing.

During my first national championship in upstate New York, I remember struggling with over-choice during one of my last sessions. Halfway through the session I opened my fly box and found myself with too many fly options. I remember slightly panicking, knowing I was racing the clock. I grabbed a fly and tied it on, only to realize it was the same fly I was just fishing. Having a pared-down selection makes it easy for me to pick a fly, and I can focus on making better drifts, approach, and reading the water.

Currently the flies that fill my fly box are much simpler. I have narrowed my selection down to a few types of flies as well as a few of my favorite patterns. It is important because I try to rely less on a specific pattern and more on getting a better drift. Here is my point: If you only have a few flies, you learn to fish them better because you do not have a choice.

Nymph fishing success often comes from our flies spending a longer time near where fish are feeding, and that is usually close to the bottom. Although our technique while fishing can be adjusted to help the flies sink, we rely on weight to get the flies to depth. Competitive angling rules restrict all weight besides what is integrated into the flies. Although we are not talking about competitive angling here, I still like to follow some of the rules while fishing.

The elimination of split shot can decrease accidental tangles. Split shot can knot quickly during a cast or hook set, and tangling is especially bad when fishing multiple flies. The split shot can also create a disconnect to the flies, making it more difficult to see soft bites when the split shot is constantly rubbing the bottom. Maintaining a connection throughout the drift helps us understand what the fly is doing under the water. When a split shot falls quickly to the bottom, it often bumps into rocks, which is detected as movement in our sighter.

I wish I could really hit the point home to everyone reading this book on how soft a fish takes the fly sometimes. If anglers can just see more bites, they

Weight adjustment is crucial to nymph fishing success. I always carry my confidence flies in various bead sizes. A Walt's Worm tied with the same profile and shape but with different bead sizes gives the angler a good assortment of weight options: 2.0, 2.3, 2.8, 3.0, 3.2, 3.5, or 3.8 mm.

Joe likes to keep his flies organized by bead size and weight in his fly box. Each side of the box is filled with flies with the same bead-head size. He carries fly boxes with the same fly patterns but in different weights. One box has smaller-size beads (2.0–2.8 mm) and the other has larger (3.2–4.0 mm).

have more opportunities to catch more fish. I will talk about bites later in this book; it takes a trained eye to see the softest takes.

Weight built directly into the fly will help us stay connected. Connection between the angler and the flies is a vital part of euro nymphing. We now can read our drift better and detect when the flies encounter anything while fishing. Not all water and fishing spots require the same weight, so it is important to have multiple weight options.

Weight is important to a good drift and should be easily adjustable. A heavier-weighted fly can help us slow down the presentation when needed. Sometimes a slower drift is what the fish seem to prefer. Switching to a lighter fly can help slow down the sink rate if the fish are eating higher in the column. Adjustments are important and need to be accurate. Knowing what weight of fly you are using and keeping the flies organized will allow you to be more efficient and understand the drift better. Weighted flies help us adjust depth and speed of the drift with a simple fly change.

The weight of a fly comes from either the bead or lead wrapped around the shank of the hook as it is being created. The weight in most of my fly patterns comes solely from a tungsten bead. I use tungsten beads of varied sizes for an assortment of weight options. Larger bead sizes equal more weight added to the fly. The material in tungsten beads is more dense and heavier than brass beads. Brass bead-heads do not give a fly much weight at all. One problem is that not all tungsten beads of the same size will be the same weight. Beads from different manufacturers and even the same company with a different batch can vary in weight. For this reason, I rely on my adjustments in weight by the diameter of the bead.

The second option for weight is adding lead when the fly is being tied. Tiers will wrap varied sizes of lead wire around the shank of the hook to make it heavier. Tying your own flies makes it possible to create micro weight adjustments. For example, you could tie a fly with a 3 mm bead with no wraps of lead, 5 wraps of lead, or 10 wraps of lead. This would give a single fly three weight options. I have limited the use of lead for a few reasons in most of my flies, and instead rely on the tungsten bead and my technique to get the fly to depth.

Weighted flies open more places that we can effectively fish. For example, when fishing an indicator setup with split shot, it is hard to make a quick connection in fast, shallow water. There would be a delay in connection until the indicator and flies catch up with the current. When using weighted flies, the angler is in more direct contact with the fly. If anything contacts the fly, the tension will be quickly detected. A weighted fly fished under a dry dropper can be super effective.

Although some assortments in weights are available, it is difficult for non-tying anglers to find fly patterns tied in every weight. Anglers who tie their own

I always like to have a fly-tying setup with me when I travel and guide. Adjustments to my flies' size, weight, and type can help when I see different situations I am trying to overcome. Tying your own flies can help you better understand drifts and weight changes or even make more precise adjustments while fishing.

flies are at an advantage because they can tie a greater variety of weights. Having the ability to tie and adjust the pattern and weight as needed can be so beneficial.

There are some situations where I will use a heavier fly called an anchor fly. The word *anchor* might be misleading to some extent. Rarely for me is the goal to have the flies hit or anchor on the bottom; usually it is to get *near* the bottom. It can be challenging to get flies quickly to the bottom to where the fish are feeding; the anchor fly could help. Anchor flies can be any fly pattern tied in a heavier weight to help get deeper quickly.

Anchor flies weigh heavier than the flies I regularly use. The word *anchor* might also make an angler visualize a large fly, but it does not need to be. Large or small, the point is they are sometimes needed, for instance when water is deep and fast. A small-profile fly with a larger bead can sometimes be all you need to get down to the strike zone. This is one reason Perdigon flies have become a staple for euro nymphing. A thin fly with an oversize bead will sink very quickly.

Teammate and friend Sean Crocker shared with me a trick while using anchor flies. We were fishing a beautiful small river winding through a little canyon in north Georgia. The water was cold, and most of the fish were not biting. The fish that were in the deeper, slow-moving pools were easy to catch. This was because it was easy to get a slow drift in water that was already slow. A slow drift gave the fish a chance to move to eat the fly. But the mountain stream consisted mostly of swift water. Sean showed me a way to get the flies to go really slow—actually not move at all—which gave the fish loads of time to move over to get the fly.

What Sean would do is use an overweight anchor fly to quickly get to the bottom. His goal was to have that heavy anchor fly sit in place on the bottom. He was using a two-fly setup with a small dropper fly attached to the tag end of a blood knot. The fly was around 20 inches up the tippet from the point fly. The point fly at the bottom was the heavy anchor fly wrapped in a lot of lead. These flies he called a throwaway fly, and he quickly tied it with simple materials. When the anchor fly stopped on the bottom, the tag fly that was suspended above the anchored fly would hold in the current. He would strategically cast the setup slightly upstream of where he thought the fish were holding. The dangling tag fly hanging in the current would entice the pickiest fish at times. He created a way to get flies to move very slowly toward the fish that were sitting underneath fast water. This is one unique situation that does not often happen, but a good angler needs to have an open mindset to be flexible and prepared to adjust.

Anglers often get stuck casting the same weight over and over. At first, it is hard to know when to change weight—do I go lighter or go heavier? Are we looking for the flies to crawl slowly near the bottom? Do we need the flies to sink slowly because the fish are sitting higher in the water column?

I think for most anglers, including myself at times, it is difficult to tell the size of a bead by just looking at it—especially because the bead sizes are close in diameter. A cool trick to keep bead sizes organized so we can distinguish the size is to put a stripe across the back of the beads with a Sharpie marker. I put a black or different-colored stripe on every other bead size. For example, 2.3 mm gets a black Sharpie, 2.5 mm I do not mark, 2.8 mm gets a red Sharpie, and so on. That trick can help you know what bead sizes you have.

There are many reasons to tie flies, but having the ability to change fly weight while using the same pattern can be a crucial one. Weight changes put the responsibility on the angler to adjust to changing conditions or circumstances. In turn these weight adjustments relay valuable feedback to the angler through fly connection and drift correction. It is important to strike a balance with weight—too much and the fly drags on bottom, too little and the fly never sinks to the fish (see more on this in Chapter 6).

FLY PROFILES

The fly's profile might be something that can be overlooked, but it can be important in some situations. The shape of a fly affects how it sinks through the water. The shape is what

we refer to as a "profile." The profile and size of a fly will also affect how fast the fly will get to the bottom. A small fly with a thin profile will cut through the water quickly and descend to the bottom with less resistance. For example, let us take two flies, both the same weights. Both have a 3 mm sized bead. One is size 10 and the other is size 18. Which one will sink faster? The smaller fly will sink faster because the smaller profile creates less drag and resistance in the water. Anglers should carry an assortment of nymphs in small and large profiles.

When targeting numbers of trout, I gravitate to using smaller flies. When targeting larger fish, a larger fly might be enough to entice a smart old fish to emerge from a hiding spot. Although large fish can be taken on small flies, an

When anglers approach fast-looking water, oftentimes they feel the need to fish heavy flies. Flies that are heavy get through the fast water on the surface but can also quickly hit the bottom. When flies hit the bottom, it becomes difficult to see soft or quick bites. Also, there are many times when fish are not sitting on the bottom. Flies with a thin profile will sink quickly without having to use extra weight. SARAH MILLER

angler's overall numbers will be reduced by only using large flies. Most of my fly patterns are on the smaller side. In most streams there seems to be more small bugs than larger ones. Fish see smaller bugs drifting by on average more than large ones. Fish are more likely not to spook from a smaller fly that drifts past.

Looking under rocks and taking a quick survey of the bugs can help you determine the general size and profile. Big flies can help draw out a big fish and be a blank saver when water is super cold. When to use large flies and small flies can be situational. It can change monthly, weekly, or sometimes even daily. Water conditions, fishing pressure, available food, and fish density can all play a role in what fish are comfortable eating.

For example, a fly in a larger profile will help during dirty or high-water conditions. The larger profile might help fish see the outline of the bug when visibility is low. Large flies can also be used to entice a smart fish from a hard-to-reach spot. Sometimes the largest or smartest fish sit in spots where drifting is almost impossible.

A few years back I was fishing a larger river filled with boulders and crazy water currents in Wyoming. The water was clear but seemed to be high in volume. The underwater substrate was lined with irregular-size rocks that made for strange currents and boils. I spotted a large brown holding about 3 feet deep near the bottom, nearly facing downstream in the churning underwater boil. The surface speed where it was sitting almost looked like a wave. I could see the fish surfing the spot and moving up and down in the crazy current. I tried but could not get my flies to slow down enough to sink to the fish, or even get in the same line as the big brown. No matter what I did I could not get a drift past this fish. I tried changing my rod angle, tuck casting, and changing weight. Plain and simple, the fish was in a hard spot. I next tried a larger-profile stonefly nymph. Knowing the large profile would be swept downstream even more quickly in the crazy fast currents, I thought the temptation of a large meal would get the fish to move. After a few casts and adjustments in sink rate, I finally cast much farther upstream, and received some help with a Colorado drift, to get the fly to sink enough to pass near the fish. The fish moved out of its spot and crushed the fly. Pretty cool to see all that go down! The point of the story is that sometimes larger flies can help get fish to move from a spot that is difficult, where a drift is about impossible.

CONFIDENCE FLIES

What flies should an angler use when they start their fishing day on the water? Hard fishing conditions, new water, or just generally a new angler can make it hard to pick what fly they should be using. Here are the fly choices I always start with, which I call confidence flies. Luckily, it has become a simple and easy choice for me. I always start with my confidence flies.

A confidence fly is not a specific fly; it can be any pattern that you enjoy fishing and believe in. There are many ways to gain confidence in your flies. Sometimes confidence in a fly can come from a local fishing legend sharing his favorite pattern, an article you read online or a YouTube video, or it could be your friend's choice. If world angler Pat Weiss told me to fish a fly that I have never fished before during a national championship, I would without hesitation because I trust his expertise and ability.

When fishing is tough, I focus on my presentation and rely on my confidence patterns to help me catch fish.

For some anglers, gaining confidence can take years of practice catching fish and other times coming home empty-handed. Catching fish on a pattern is sometimes all it takes, but that can take time. Your confidence patterns might also change or evolve over the years. The flies I had confidence in five years ago look different from the flies I am confident in today. I now tie some of the flies in thinner profiles, or with a different goal in mind. *As our fishing progresses, our fly patterns evolve.*

Every time you are out on the water is a new opportunity to gain confidence in specific patterns for different situations. If I am fishing a stream filled with pocketwater holding wild browns, I will fish a size 16 Walt's Worm with confidence. Trust in the Walt's Worm was built from many positive past experiences fishing similar water types for wild trout.

Having confidence is important while fishing (obviously, confidence is important in anything you do). The longer a fly is fished, the more fish it will pass. That fly will produce more fish. What I am trying to say is, the more you use a fly and catch fish, the more confidence you will have in that fly.

I believe a good presentation in most situations is just as important as the fly you are using. Getting good drifts is what we are after, and having confidence while fishing will help bring fish to the net. Cam Chioffi, a world-class angler, told me to always be confident in every cast. He told me that he expects to get a bite on every drift. Isn't that the point of making a drift, to catch a fish? I

Above: A vibrant central Pennsylvania resident falls victim to a simple Walt's Worm.

Left: A France Fly looks like the real thing.

translated his comment to mean that you should believe in what you are doing on every cast, and that having confidence is more important than having the best fly. A fly might not be the right pattern, but fished with confidence it can outfish the perfect fly fished with no confidence.

My confidence flies while euro nymphing are smaller-size nymphs. If I had to pick one size to use forever it would be size 18. A smaller nymph drifting past a fish is less intrusive than a large fly. Larger-profile flies will often catch more current than a fly that is skinnier, which will cause the fly to speed up through the drift. A faster-drifted fly might drift past the fish faster than a natural bug, spooking the fish.

I have boiled my fly choices down to three confidence patterns that have helped me produce trout in most situations. The same three patterns have been productive throughout the world, from the spring creeks of central Pennsylvania to the mountain streams of southern Chile to the waters of eastern Europe. My search for the perfect fly is slowly fading away. I will always keep an open mind as new patterns surface and techniques evolve, but as of now *a well-drifted fly is slightly more important than the pattern.*

Having a few confidence flies will help make you a well-rounded nymph angler. Limiting your fly selections, at least at first as you are developing skill and confidence, can help you focus more on technique, approach, and drift. Having confidence will help you be more successful while fishing.

Here are my top three confidence fly patterns:

- Walt's Worm
- France Fly
- Pheasant Tail (Frenchie)

ATTRACTOR FLIES

Fishing can be hard when the conditions are tough. Sometimes a cold snap or off-color water after a rain event can really make fishing a challenge. These are times when I grab my fly box that is filled with attractor flies. Attractor flies should be staple patterns for every nymph angler. An attractor is not just one specific pattern; it can be any traditional fly pattern jazzed up with bright thread, flash, or a shiny bead. These patterns can come in many styles, types, and sizes. Dedicated attractor flies like Rainbow Warriors have all the right triggers to attract fish. Added flash, a hot spot, or UV material can make it hard for a fish to ignore.

Hot spots usually are created with fluorescent or brightly colored thread that is added to the fly. Fluorescent color is thought to be more visible to trout, especially during adverse conditions. A hot spot is typically located behind the bead, just enough to add some contrast and a bright spot to the fly.

Another use for attractor flies is to help us understand the drift. A tracer fly is a highly visible fly that we can watch in the water. A brightly colored egg that is easily visible can be a good tracer fly. Its purpose is to help us watch the fly as it sinks and travels through the drift. Having the ability to see the fly will help us understand what happens through a drift. Often, we think the nymphs are upstream during the drift, but unknowingly the flies are somewhere completely different. The tracer fly will help us see the path the flies take.

There are a few times I will lean on attractor patterns. However, throughout a full year I typically will use more dull flies than attractor flies. I believe that a dull and more natural fly can be difficult for a fish to refuse. Flash, extra sparkle, and bright colors are more reasons for a fish to say no sometimes. I like to think of a simple Walt's with no hot spots or extra flash like a piece of

A few minutes after a heavy downpour, the far side of the stream was quickly becoming dirty from runoff entering from upstream. I saw this fish going nuts as the water was quickly rising. When I saw the fish and the water conditions rapidly changing, I knew I needed to make a fast choice. I decided to change to a heavier tippet and switched to an attractor fly that caught the attention of the fish before the water turned to mud. GORDON VANDERPOOL

cheese pizza. On the opposite side, a fly packed with flash is like a pizza with many toppings. Not everyone likes every topping, but most everyone would eat a plain slice of cheese pizza.

BEAD COLOR

This topic gets me excited. Who would think that the color of the bead on the fly could be so important to some fish? I can attest to times when fishing with Team USA or practicing with competitive anglers that instead of someone asking what fly the other anglers are using, they specifically ask what color is the bead? Crazy or not, some of us believe that the bead on a fly can attract or even spook fish depending on different water conditions or the target species of fish. I will go so far as to say sometimes fish will eat just a silver bead on a hook.

There are times when certain bead colors spook the trout. I have seen brown trout in spring creeks spook from my silver bead fly as it drifted near a fish. The weather, stream conditions, fish pressure, species, and bug activity can be factors in choosing what bead color to use. For me, picking an appropriate bead color comes from experience. There is no exact science to it, but it is good to have a starting point. Sometimes it is just a matter of switching colors until one works.

In 2014 I was fishing in North Carolina when I first realized the importance of different bead colors. I spent the week fishing with Gordon Vanderpool. Gordon and I fished one of his favorite rivers, a moderate-size tailwater filled with stunning wild rainbow trout. We fished a section that was flat but slightly broken with some rocks making small depressions in the river.

Gordon was catching 10 fish to my 1 during our first fishing session of the morning. He noticed I was catching fewer fish and asked me what color bead I was using. I remember thinking right away, *It is interesting that he is asking me about the bead color over the fly pattern.* So, after getting a butt kicking for a few hours, I followed his advice and switched to flies with silver beads, and, yes, I caught more fish.

Those feisty little wild rainbows on that river loved the silver bead. I could see them moving a few feet at times to investigate my flies as they passed by. Many of the rules I follow when picking a specific color bead have come from hours of fishing on the water with positive or negative results. I mentally keep a note of when I see something working well. It is important to use the results of your past successes and failures to devise a plan for what to start with and when to adjust. For example, now when I am targeting wild rainbows, my starting point is using silver-beaded flies because that has worked well in the past. Silver beads are also a good color when fishing in adverse conditions.

A little flash can go a long way in dirty water. Fishing when water visibility is low can be challenging. Sometimes all it takes is a little bit of extra flash to get a fish's attention. A silver bead is more visible in cloudy water. I can account for many days of fishing where a silver bead was enough to pull fish. I believe trout

I saw and missed this fish as it ate my silver bead Walt's Worm on the first drift through a little pocket. On the next few drifts, the fish ignored my fly. I switched to a slightly smaller Walt's with a copper bead and the fish ate on the next drift.

in some fisheries can see a lot better than we think in cloudy water. The flashy bead will reflect ambient light, which will help attract fish. Just the curiosity of something flashy can trigger fish to come and investigate. When you are unsure of where the fish are sitting, the flash of a silver-beaded fly can help you cover more areas. During the winter when the water is cold, a silver bead could similarly entice fish to investigate. During a quick cold snap or in the dead of winter, fish will sometimes pod up in tight groups, making them difficult to find.

Silver bead flies can also be a staple for me to use during a big hatch. I was fishing on the South Holston River in Tennessee during a heavy early season Blue-Winged Olive hatch. It was around March, and the water and air were still on the chilly side. Only a few fish were actively rising, especially in the shallow riffle section that I was fishing. I could see trout flashing under the surface as they ate passing BWO nymphs and emergers in the ankle-deep water.

I put on a Pheasant Tail like a Frenchie with a copper bead. The size and shape of my fly was close to the natural bugs that the fish were actively eating. After a few minutes with no bites while casting to actively eating fish, I switched bead colors from copper to silver. In my working box I had the same Frenchie fly in copper and silver beads. It only took a few casts to bring a fish to hand. I had nonstop action over the next hour or so while the hatch continued. I'm not sure why something works the way it does, but I try to go from my past experiences. A dull fly with little or no flash, hot spots, or attractors can get lost in the mix of all the natural bugs as they pass by. The flash of the silver bead might be all it takes for the fly to stand out.

When I am searching for fish, I gravitate to a two-fly setup. My confidence fly will be a copper-beaded Walt's Worm on the bottom and a silver-beaded France Fly on the top tag position in my setup. This is my go-to setup when fishing larger water, or just a good starting point in the beginning of my fishing day. It gives the fish two different options in bead colors and positions in the columns of water. I like to offer these two contrasting beaded fly colors: one flashy and one dull.

Bead Color Rules

Here is a good starting point to picking the right bead color:
- Silver bead: wild rainbows, sunny days, cloudy water, heavy hatches, cold days
- Copper bead: wild browns, overcast days, clear water, pressured fish, stocked rainbows

When fishing in fast water, my confidence and starting point is using silver-beaded flies. I like to think the flash of the silver in fast water might be enough to make the fish move or get its attention as the fly quickly passes the fish. This rainbow fell to a silver-beaded fly in fast water. ROCH MILLER

Spooky fish, spring creeks, and low water conditions can be a good time to fish with a copper-beaded fly. I think fish can get used to seeing specific fly patterns too often. Sometimes less flash can be less intrusive. Copper-beaded flies have been a staple when fishing for pressured rainbows. Soon after being stocked, rainbows can fall quickly to the sparkle of a silver bead, but they seem to wise up quickly. Sometimes a dull fly is a good starting point when fishing for spooky and pressured fish.

An important approach that my father really encouraged while I was competing was to try to be different. He would urge me to try to think and approach the water differently than my opponent. If you know everyone on the stream is fishing a copper-beaded fly, use something else. I think fish can get accustomed to seeing the same thing.

Here is one example I experienced recently. I spotted a fish sitting in the tail out of a long pool. I approached the fish slowly from straight downstream, trying to stay out of its vision. I got close enough to watch the mouth of the fish and see how it would react to my drift. On the first cast I missed the fish while using a copper-beaded fly. The next five consecutive casts I drifted the same copper-beaded fly past the fish without the fish ever even moving. I took a moment to switch to the same pattern in a silver bead head. On the first cast I watched the white flash of the fish's mouth as it ate the fly. The point is to think differently, try various things, and be willing to make adjustments!

HOOKS

The hook is the last connection between you and the fish, so make sure it is a good one. The most used hook style designed for euro nymphing techniques are jig hooks. There are a few things about hooks (without going into too much detail) that will help you pick the best style.

For me fish safety is a top priority while angling, and I encourage other anglers to take care of our fish. I recommend the use of barbless hooks not only for a quicker release of a fish but for safety and ease of removal if the hook snags our clothing or other areas. Companies like Fulling Mill and Hanak make some of the best hooks on the market. These hooks are sharp and designed to hold fish during a fight.

One key to hooks is their wire size. I realized a few years back the importance in some situations of using strong-wired hooks. I was fishing in northern Colorado with my friend Joe during the end of spring runoff. The river was flowing fast with a strong current, and the fish were happily and regularly eating.

I approached a juicy-looking run in the river immediately upstream above a set of fast-falling pocketwater. Using a Tailwater Sow Bug fly, I distinctly remember a reaction bite as the flies sank to depth. The take was obvious as the sighter moved forward, and I set the hook to witness a large brown breach a foot or two out of the water. Within a few seconds the fish turned and was already

A fly tied with a strong hook can be important when fishing in streams with fast water and hard-fighting fish. JOSH MILLER

headed downstream through fast pocketwater. The fight ended quickly, and the line went slack. I disappointedly retrieved my line, expecting the fly to be gone. To my surprise the fly was still there, but after a quick inspection I noticed that the hook was bent out. I cut off the fly and switched to another, and within a few hours I lost another large brown trout the same way.

I learned the hard way that in some streams, conditions, or situations it is important to use a hook with good strong wire. However, when fishing small streams with smaller fish, there are other benefits to using a hook with thinner wire.

A few friends who are world-level competitors often euro nymph with flies tied on dry-fly hooks, which are manufactured with a superthin wire. The benefit is the thin wire will quickly and easily pierce a fish. A soft hook set is all that is needed to hook a fish, which gives anglers the ability to use very fine-diameter tippets. However, if you hook a hot fish in big water, you risk bending out that hook in a hurry. I will use different hook sizes depending on water conditions or the fish size I am after. I like to nymph with jig hooks and nymph hooks that have a fairly straight point. I think a straight point hook will pierce and hold a fish well. Also check the points of your hooks to make sure they have not rounded over after hitting a few rocks while fishing. Dull hooks are not good!

THE FLIES

WALT'S WORM

Originated by Walt Young; tied by Josh Miller

Hook: #18 dry fly
Bead: Copper 2.3 mm tungsten slotted bead
Thread: Olive 8/0
Rib: Thread
Body: Natural rabbit dubbing
Note: I use rabbit dubbing fur in a neutral tan color. Other colors include olive, mustard, and gray. Natural fur blended with synthetic and including a light mixture of flash can create a good-looking fly.

JIG WALT'S WORM

Originated by Walt Young; tied by Josh Miller

Hook: #18 jig

Bead: Silver 2.5 mm tungsten slotted bead
Thread: Olive 8/0
Body: Natural rabbit dubbing

FRANCE FLY

Originated by Hunter Hoffler and US Youth team; tied by Nick Meloy

Hook: #16 jig
Bead: Silver 2.4 mm tungsten slotted bead
Thread: Black 8/0
Body: Black micro tubing
Tail: Dark Pardo CDL tailing fibers
Note: Slightly stretching the tubing can help keep the body slim or create a slight taper. I also use olive, tan, and clear tubing material. Clear is a good choice that can be tied over various thread colors, giving the fly a slight translucent appearance.

FRENCHIE

Originated by Lance Egan; tied by Lance Egan

Hook: #16 jig
Bead: Gold 2.5 mm tungsten slotted bead
Thread: Red 8/0
Rib: Copper wire
Body: Natural pheasant tail and shrimp pink dubbing
Tail: Dark Pardo CDL tailing fibers

OG FRENCHIE

Originated by Lance Egan; tied by Josh Miller

Hook: #16 jig
Bead: Copper 2.5 mm tungsten slotted bead
Thread: Red 8/0
Rib: Red wire
Body: Natural pheasant tail
Tail: Dark Pardo CDL tailing fibers

THREAD FRENCHIE

Originated by Lance Egan; tied by Lance Egan

Hook: #16 jig
Bead: Gold 2.5 mm tungsten slotted bead
Thread: Olive 8/0
Rib: Copper wire
Body: Pink dubbing
Tail: Dark Pardo CDL tailing fibers

ZONE STONE

Originated by Josh Miller; tied by Josh Miller

Hook: #14 jig
Bead: Copper 2.8 mm tungsten slotted bead
Thread: Olive 6/0
Body: Black micro tubing and gold and brown Ice Dub
Tail: Golden turkey biots

RAINBOW WARRIOR

Originated by Lance Egan; tied by Derek Hathazy
Hook: #16 jig
Bead: Silver 2.5 mm tungsten slotted bead
Thread: Red 8/0
Body: Pearl tinsel and Rainbow Scud Dub
Tail: Dark Pardo CDL tailing fibers

TAILWATER SOW BUG

Originated by Lance Egan; tied by Ken Crane
Hook: #16 jig
Bead: Silver 2.5 mm tungsten slotted bead
Thread: Red 8/0
Rib: Silver wire
Body: Rainbow Scud Dub

OLIVE WARRIOR

Originated by Lance Egan; tied by Jess Westbrook
Hook: #18 jig
Bead: Copper 2.3 mm tungsten slotted bead
Thread: Olive 8/0
Body: Pearl tinsel and olive dubbing
Tail: Dark Pardo CDL tailing fibers

HOT BUTT PERDIGON

Tied by Erik Clymore
Hook: #16 jig
Bead: Silver 2.8 mm tungsten slotted bead
Thread: Black and red 8/0
Body: Pearl tinsel coated with UV epoxy
Tail: Dark Pardo CDL tailing fibers

WEISS' SIMPLE PTN

Originated by Pat Weiss; tied by Eric Kelley

Hook: #16 jig
Bead: Copper 2.5 mm tungsten slotted bead
Thread: Tan 8/0
Rib: Small Gold wire
Tail: Pheasant tail

BREAD-N-BUTTER NYMPH

Originated by Domenick Swentosky; tied by Domenick Swentosky

Hook: Jig or standard nymph style #10-16
Bead: Gold tungsten bead
Thread: Brown 8/0 Uni-Thread
Rib: Small Gold wire
Abdomen: Hareline Dubbin Hare's Ear
Thorax: Arizona Synthetic Peacock (Bronze)
Collar: Rust Brown 8/0 Uni-Thread
Tail: Coq de Leon, Dark Pardo

SIMPLE SULFUR

Originated by Josh Miller; tied by Tim Cammisa

Hook: #16 jig
Bead: Copper 2.5 mm tungsten slotted bead
Thread: Red 8/0
Rib: Red Sulky
Body: Brown rabbit and fluorescent orange Wapsi Super Fine Dubbing
Tail: Dark Pardo CDL tailing fibers

MICRO EGG

Originated by Pat Weiss; tied by Josh Miller

Hook: #18 jig
Bead: Copper 2.5 mm tungsten slotted bead
Thread: Red 8/0
Body: Early Girl McFlyfoam

JDK

Originated by Josh Miller; tied by Lewis Hersch

Hook: #16 jig

Bead: Silver 2.5 mm tungsten slotted bead

Thread: Olive 8/0

Body: Blue holographic tinsel

Tail: Light Pardo CDL tailing fibers

LITTLE J BUG

Originated by Sean Crocker; tied by Sean Crocker

Hook: #16 jig

Bead: Copper 2.4 mm tungsten slotted bead

Body: Olive 8/0 thread coated with UV epoxy

Tail: Medium Pardo CDL tailing fibers

Here I am focused on my drift while using a lightweight leader and small flies. RODGER OBLEY

Former US Youth world team member Mike Komara adapts his cast to productively fish this water. Not all situations will allow overhead and common casting methods. Great anglers can adjust their technique to fish in any condition the river presents.

5

Casting

Casting is an art form that is used to help anglers get flies to where fish live and to present those flies as naturally as possible. The gear and setup for euro nymphing is slightly different from traditional fly fishing, and the casts vary a bit as well. Although some of the mechanics of a cast will be similar, some euro nymphing casts are different. The casts and techniques we use are a result of fishing with lighter flies, longer and lighter leaders, and thinner line. It is important to adapt our approach as we implement more technical drifts, work harder-to-fish places, and use specialized gear.

For example, when I tell my students that we will be using a leader that is 18 feet or longer, it sounds intimidating to some. Luckily, some casts are simple and tailored to fishing longer leaders. The biggest difference is that some euro casts use the weight of the fly to cast and not the fly line.

When casting a traditional fly rod, the rod will load and cast under the weight of the fly line. When fishing with a euro nymphing setup, the thin and light fly line creates minimal load on the rod to cast. We rely on the weight of the leader and flies to load and cast. With a lightweight leader and flies, there is less weight to help load and cast a rod. A solution is to use water loading to help us cast. Water loading creates tension on the leader and flies. The water will try to hold back our fly as we cast because of the water tension on the fly. This resistance will help bend and load the rod like using more weight. You can use water loading on both the

Devin Olsen is deadly accurate with his setup. Accuracy is important to effectively cover every potential holding spot, such as in this sick pocketwater stretch of river. RUSSELL MILLER

forward and reverse parts of a cast. Water loading will help you increase power, distance, and accuracy.

I like to use a mix of overhead and low-angle casts while fishing. Some casts seem to fit better in certain scenarios. Using an overhead-style cast like the quarter cast can help anglers with accuracy, but for a beginner it can get you tangled in a hurry. Windy conditions will quickly affect the flies and leader as they arch overhead, decreasing accuracy, especially with light leaders with a downstream wind. This is when the Frisbee cast with a low rod angle can be effective.

The Frisbee cast partnered with the 180 rule uses a low rod angle to keep the leader and flies in a straight line. Casts like the roll cast are less effective with light leaders when the leader goes high into the air, losing power and accuracy. If you are coming from a traditional fly-fishing background, this new kind of casting can be frustrating and awkward at first. With practice and repetition, you will get better and end up catching more fish.

It will take time to learn new casting movements and to forget some of the muscle memory from traditional casts. Often I will show a cast to a student and it works well for them. However, within a short period of time they revert back to traditional casting movements. Muscle memory can kick in as we practice getting good drifts.

Before we get into the details about the types of casts, remember—a good cast sets up a good drift. I tell my students that a good cast is the foundation to every good drift. There are many ways to cast a fly to the target, but there are a few casts that work better. Fishing more challenging drifts is harder to accomplish without a good cast and proper technique. Lastly, slow down while casting. Take your time; it's not a race.

The following instructions on casting were difficult to write. Sometimes simple concepts can be complex to explain. I tried to picture what I wanted to say and put it into words. However, I learned that the best way to write it down was by just pretending I was on the water talking directly to a student.

180 RULE

Accuracy is key to any good cast. Casts that are accurate help anglers be more efficient while fishing, covering a stream quickly and more effectively without wasting time with inaccurate casts. An accurate cast is also important because a misplaced cast could spook fish.

As leaders have evolved to become lighter and longer, our casts and approach also have changed. Wind and light flies make it harder to be accurate. Accuracy comes with practice, but the technique we call the 180 rule will help you be more precise with your cast.

The 180 rule means that wherever our fly is placed downstream in the water before a cast, the flies will land 180 degrees from that spot. Another way to describe it is that wherever the target area is upstream, the flies should be anchored 180 degrees in the opposite direction downstream. After the flies are settled in the water directly downstream, draw an imaginary line from the flies through the fly rod. The line should then continue straight to the path where the flies will be cast.

On the backcast, place the flies downstream in the water. The flies need to be tightly connected through the leader to the rod tip to make a cast. Moving the rod tip to either side will help position the flies directly opposite of the upstream target. To cast across to the stream bank, put the flies behind you toward the opposite stream bank. The 180 rule is a straight-line cast. The fastest way between two points is a straight line. This is our objective, especially while using the Frisbee cast, to keep our flies in a straight line from point to point.

When fishing with a light leader you will quickly find out that it is very difficult to change the direction of the cast. The flies naturally travel in a straight line from where the flies are anchored in the water. This scenario is when the 180 rule will be beneficial. Take the time to position the flies downstream or upstream, depending on what direction you are casting. Also take the time to set up a good anchoring placement, which will help with precision and a more accurate cast. The leader should be tightly connected with the flies and the rod tip low as you start to make the cast.

FRISBEE CAST

Small streams choked with overhanging trees can make it very difficult to cast. A good number of the trout streams that I frequently fish in Pennsylvania either have a low canopy of trees or some kind of obstacle. With casts like a traditional roll cast, the leader and flies often end up in the trees. A low-angle cast can help keep our flies low enough to pass under the trees.

After many days of fishing frustration, the Frisbee cast was created. It was a great solution to help us fish streams that are tight with overhead cover. The cast helps keep our flies and leader low, avoiding brush and trees. The cast also has enough power to move through the wind and far under low-hanging structures where the fish often lurk.

Fish like to sit in places that are hard to reach. Here I use a Frisbee cast to launch my flies deep under the brush on a limestone influenced stream in central Pennsylvania where trout are hiding. ROGER OBLEY

Joe Clark and I have been actively fishing and teaching euro nymphing on streams in Pennsylvania for many years. The Frisbee cast partnered with the 180 rule was a natural adjustment for us when we needed a way to fish streams choked with trees. There were many times I would spot some trout freely eating under an overhanging structure that was seemingly impossible to reach. As anglers we need to be able to adapt to our environment. How we fish and our approach need to be changeable. The Frisbee cast came from time on the water trying to overcome these obstacles to cast to fish that are not often targeted.

Euro nymphing and wind are two things that do not go great hand in hand. To make it worse, light flies and leaders are easily affected by overhead casts, making accuracy and distance challenging. The low angle of the Frisbee cast helps cut through the wind better. The wind is stronger the higher you get above the water. For this reason, overhead casts are more affected by wind than casts closer to the water. The Frisbee cast keeps the flies close to the water in a straight line as they travel to their destination. If needed, you can be forceful and deliberate with the Frisbee cast to power through a heavy breeze.

To Frisbee cast, start with the flies anchored in the water downstream. Keep in mind the 180 rule. The key to the cast is to keep the fly rod traveling in a straight line throughout its course. The flies will also travel in a straight line as they move toward the destination.

Where the cast can go wrong is when the angler breaks their wrist in a circular motion similar to a roll cast. Whatever path the fly rod takes, the leader and flies follow. So if the fly rod lifts during a cast, the flies will lift too. Try to keep the rod level during the cast.

I notice for some anglers it can be difficult to maintain a level cast, and to not revert back to roll casting. It is so ingrained in anglers because a roll cast is used when fishing with indicators and fly line. However, I see accuracy and distance decline when the muscle memory of motions like a roll cast slowly creeps back in. Try to keep the rod low and traveling in a straight line.

Explaining the cast can be challenging, and this is why Joe Clark produced the name Frisbee cast, also known as a tip cast. He told me it was easier for his students to grasp the movement of the cast by the name Frisbee. Back-handed and forward-handed casts are similar to how we would throw a Frisbee. This can be done with the forearm but mostly with the use of the wrist.

Next, anchor the flies on either the forward or back part of the cast. Remember the 180 rule. The fastest distance between two points is a straight line, so anchor your flies directly downstream of your target. Make sure the leader is always tightly connected to your flies as they are anchored in the water. It is important to have connection to the flies before starting the cast.

Square up your body and shoulders to the target. Stand tall and use good posture. Remember to keep your eyes on the target. Slowly move the tip of the fly rod toward the target to lift the fly to the surface as you start the cast. The cast should be a slow movement with your forearm traveling toward the destination until the flies are on the surface. The slow movement will also start to load the fly rod.

Once the flies have traveled to the surface, use a level flicking movement of your wrist, casting the flies toward the destination. The flick is important because it will load the rod and accelerate the flies to cast. Timing is key to flick right when the flies are at the surface. Flicking too early will prevent the flies from casting with full power. Flicking the flies too late means the rod has already moved too far toward the target. To summarize the movements, the cast consists of a slow acceleration ending with an aggressive wrist flick keeping the rod low and level to cast the flies to the target. A recent student said the flick is similar to a snapshot in hockey, or if someone was trying to get paint off a paintbrush.

I watched legendary fly angler Bob Clouser as he gave a casting demo at the New Jersey Fly Fishing Show. He was demonstrating a few different casts while using a traditional fly line. The cast that caught my eye was one where he was casting a weighted fly. The part that was most interesting was casting from his hip and keeping the fly under the rod tip during the cast. I remember him saying that he usually tried to keep the fly under the tip when using flies with weight. Similarly, the Frisbee cast will keep the flies and leader under or directly at the fly rod tip.

One main point I want to stress in this book is to slow down and take your time—not only with casting, but with everything you do while fly fishing. Take your time to place the flies exactly where you want them downstream before casting. When an angler starts to pick up the tempo and does not take the extra moment to water-load their flies, oftentimes day-ending tangles can happen. Slow down, determine the target, place the flies 180 degrees in the water opposite to the target, and then cast.

Using deliberate motions during each cast is important for the flies to make it to their destination. A weak cast can get tangled easily. However, an overpowered cast could bounce backward, reducing the distance of the cast.

The Frisbee cast will help set us up for a few slightly more technical drifts, such as gaining immediate connection. One more trick to get a quick connection: After the cast, raise the rod immediately to keep the sighter from ever hitting the water.

QUARTER CAST

Accuracy and connection while casting can help us catch more fish. I had a recent discussion about being instantly connected to the flies with an angler whom I admire greatly. We both agreed that in some situations, anglers could catch up to 50 percent more fish if they could get in connection faster to their flies immediately after the cast.

The quarter cast is an effective way to place the flies upstream with precision and fast connection. I like to use the quarter cast when fishing directly upstream in shallow water. It is also a great way to fish slightly across the stream, or quartering, as the name suggests.

Accuracy is based on the correct execution of the cast. Square up to the target. Rotate the rod slightly behind your head up to your ear, like you are answering the phone. Let the flies settle under the rod tip as they hang behind your back. Look down the rod and rotate your wrist toward the target. The flies should

The quarter cast is great when the angler wants to use a high rod angle, especially to slow down the flies in sections of river like these shallow, short pockets. ROGER OBLEY

rotate around the rod in a large and connected arch. Stop the rod high, allowing the flies to dip into the water with minimal extra slack. Connection will happen very quickly depending on how high you stop the rod. The rod might need to be stopped even higher in shallow, quick water. Because the leader and flies rotate up into the air during the cast, this approach is not the best choice in streams with low canopy. For that reason, too, wind will affect accuracy, especially while fishing lightweight leaders.

TUCK CAST

A heavier fly will sink quickly to the zone, but sometimes a heavy fly is not what the fish want. The tuck cast will help get lighter-weight flies to sink more quickly. Water depth and where the fish are can change at any time. Even in the same run, there could be many different depths of water where the fish are eating. This cast offers depth adjustability without having to change the weight of the fly. Lighter flies can get better drifts, but they can be harder to control and get to depth.

The ability to manipulate our casts is another reason euro nymph fishing is so versatile and productive. We can alter our approach and technique to fish different waters without having to change our setup. The tuck cast gives anglers the ability to fish different depths and water columns with the same fly. It can be combined

The tuck cast helps get flies to sink faster without using more weight. Often used in deeper water, sometimes a reduced tuck cast can be productive in shallow water. JOE CLARK

with other styles of casting like the Frisbee casting method. The first time I heard about the tuck cast was from fly-fishing legend George Daniel. How the flies enter the water during the cast can help or limit how much the flies will sink. A controlled but overpowered cast will push the flies into the water by turning the leader over. A brisk acceleration to an exaggerated stop of the fly rod tip is what forces the flies into the water. The speed that the flies enter the water helps drive the flies through the current and gets them to sink quickly. A high and abrupt stop of the rod accelerates the flies into the water from a vertical angle.

Slack is another part of this cast that can be controlled to also help get the flies to sink. Slack is what gives the flies more freedom to sink with less resistance. Greater amounts of slack allow the flies a longer time to sink; however, too much slack equals loss of connection. Part of developing this technique is finding balance in slack. Try to get the tippet to land directly on top of where the flies have landed, or slightly upstream. This will create the slack needed for the flies to sink.

Extra slack can be achieved if the angler drifts the rod forward toward the casting destination immediately after the rod tip stops during the cast. Even though slack is involved, it is important to stay connected to the flies to detect a take. The next variable to control depth is time. The longer the angler gives the slack, the deeper the fly will sink (this will be talked about more in depth in Chapter 6).

Instead of taking the time to change weight, we can simply adjust our cast to sink the fly. Not every fishing spot is the same. The tuck cast is a cool way for anglers to fish in more depths and water types without changing their setup.

BOW AND ARROW CAST

Fishing around obstacles like trees and brush can make casting exceedingly difficult. Casting can be especially hard when there is limited or no backcasting room to anchor the flies. The bow and arrow cast helps us fish streams that are tightly choked with brush. It is also a good cast to get the flies under a tree or structure even when fishing a large stream. Usually, the cast works best and most accurately from 10 to 20 feet. Sometimes, if you can get the fly in these hard-to-reach places, the fish are very willing to eat. Learn the bow and arrow cast; it will help you become a better-rounded angler.

Here Joe Clark uses the bow and arrow cast when traditional casts would be difficult. The bow and arrow is an effective way to get the flies to places that can be hard to reach. The cast is great on small streams but also just as effective when fishing the banks and obstacles on larger rivers.

Pennsylvania native Joe Humphreys is a master of the bow and arrow cast. I watched Joe teach the US Youth team this cast while fishing a small brook trout stream in Clinton County in Pennsylvania. The stream was super tight, overgrown, and with little room to cast. Joe easily and precisely placed his flies in tight places with a bow and arrow cast. He was able to catch trout from spots where a traditional cast would have been impossible.

To learn the bow and arrow cast, start by having the same amount of leader out as the length of the fly rod. Hold the bottom fly (using a one-fly setup with this cast is preferable). Grab that fly behind the bend of the hook with your thumb and first finger. Be mindful of the hook point. Holding the rod at arm level, firmly point the rod at the target. Pull the fly toward you by raising your arm and flexing the fly rod. Pull backward toward your head then slightly to the side until you have bent the fly rod. Release the fly carefully but hold the rod steady as you keep your eyes focused on the target.

Use the bow and arrow cast to open more fishing opportunities and places that are difficult to reach with a fly.

Each section of water, time of year, and varying water levels can fish differently. The same approach and technique might not be the best for every situation. Use your playbook of techniques to test and sample the water to help figure out the best way to produce fish. JOE CLARK

6

Bring It All Together

Now it is time to bring it all together. Since my focus is no longer primarily on fly patterns, I can focus on developing technique and instinct. Think of euro nymphing like football: You are the coach and need to call the plays. Good coaches have a large playbook for what they see on the field. We also need to have a large playbook while fishing different situations and conditions. Fly fishing is a game of skill, and the fish are the goal. In fly fishing we have the tools (as described in previous chapters) to help create our plays. As in football, we assess the field and weigh our options. We gravitate to certain plays because they work. Euro nymphing gives us versatility to adjust each technique as needed. Anglers need to develop great control over the drift while using their specialized gear. Elements such as speed, depth, and rod angles are just a few important skills we need to learn to work with conditions the river throws at us. The drift—how the flies move through the water—is the execution of the play to reach our goal. We can change how the flies drift by manipulating our approach. After understanding the choices and variables for a drift, we need to know how to put it all together.

UNDERSTANDING DRIFT

A drift is simply the space between when your fly hits the water on a cast and when it leaves. In theory it's simple, but in reality so much can happen during a drift

After my first few casts fishing higher in the water column, I gave the flies slack to help them sink for a second at the start of the drift. This fish surprised me as it took the flies almost immediately as they sank. Take note of little details as you miss and catch fish to help you adjust your approach. ROCH MILLER

that can improve or reduce your chances of catching a fish. There is a balance in adjusting with our drifts, controlling variables such as slack, tempo, and rod angle rather than physically changing the setup's weight or tippet to physically change depth. Not all drifts are the same, as unique styles, techniques, and approaches are needed to feed the flies to the fish in creative ways.

For example, "floating the sighter" is a drift technique often used when fishing in shallow water. This technique helps us stay connected with a lighter fly at a distance to help see takes. It also allows the fly to fall more naturally through the water column with less tension, a key aspect to achieving a smooth sink rate. Through the years it has surprised me how many fish I have caught when the flies are just falling or sinking to depth. Knowing a variety of drifting techniques helps anglers find the fish.

The more experience you have catching or missing fish, the more you will start to understand behavior and fish habits. Most of my students during guided trips are shocked at some of the places they catch fish. If my goal is to catch more fish that session, it makes sense to maximize our efforts and cast over the *eating* fish.

Fish can hold throughout the water at different times, but the constant is that they will almost always eat naturally drifted food. During that entire time, in theory, a fish could eat your presentation at any point. So connection and strike detection visually is important. Connection comes with control over the drift, which takes time and practice. The goal of a drift is usually to get the flies to act as naturally as possible as they travel through the water.

We need to *always* be aware of drag and the constant battle to regulate. Drag happens when water pushes against the setup. It speeds up our flies as they drift through the water. The pressure against the line and flies speeds up the presentation, making it appear unnatural to the fish. When fish are actively eating, a drift with drag as the flies move quickly downstream could still catch fish. But overall, we want to have as much control over drag as possible for times when fish are pickier. Floating indicators on a traditional setup with a larger surface area are even more at the mercy of the surface speed of the water. Oftentimes anglers will try to overcome drag with the use of more weight. Again, the goal of the drift is to present flies as naturally as possible.

When fishing pocket-type water, especially in colder months, the speed of the drift can be especially important. Fish can be lazy as their metabolism slows down in the cold-water months. Getting the flies to almost stall out during the drift is my mindset for the approach. Conversely, in the summer the trout can be shockingly fast to eat a fly in quick water. A heavily leading technique just to maintain connection could be the ticket.

It is important to adjust the rod angle to present the flies at different speeds to the fish. Here I use a vertical angle to help slow down the presentation when the fish are acting stubbornly. The stream bottom can also be very contoured, and it can be about impossible to get flies directly in front of the fish. A slower drift will give the flies more time in the pocket, hopefully making it harder for them to resist. JOE CLARK

When fish are very active, euro anglers often have much better success. It could be because active fish are more inclined to move and eat almost anything that passes by. When fish are actively eating, anglers can be successful with unpolished technique. Last season I fished an evening with a friend who was unknowingly drifting with excessive amounts of drag. However, he was still catching a respectable number of fish. The drawback is that his success could be misleading and solidify improper or unknowing technique. When both fish and bugs are active, fish can be less drift sensitive. The fish that day did not seem to mind the inexperienced angler not slowing down or controlling the drift very well. The next time the angler fished the same location, he did not have the same success.

The lesson of this story is it is easy for anglers to blame the fish and say, "They're just not eating," when there could be more to it. These are times when anglers might then rely on switching the fly pattern when, instead, they should slow down or adjust the drift. If you want to advance to a higher level and catch more fish, start by changing your technique mindset.

When euro nymph fishing, the sighter is the tool we use to gauge our drift speed. I like to call it a "book" that gives us lots of data on what is going on. The sighter is the piece of highly visible material attached at the end of the leader, placed between the leader and the tippet. The material is soft and sensitive, which helps us detect anything that encounters our flies as they drift.

When euro nymphing and fly fishing in general, it is important to *visually see* what we are doing. If you cannot see, it makes it extremely harder to catch. The sighter also helps us detect bites and "read our drift." We should be constantly looking for any movement in the sighter, which would indicate a bite. The position of the sighter helps us understand what the flies are doing underneath the water. We can manipulate the sighter's angle with our fly rod, which will alter how the flies sink and drift. The use of many sighter angle positions offers an extensive number of adjustments we can effectively use in all types of water.

When a fish eats the fly, we detect it through the sighter by both sight and feel. Visually we detect bites or the bottom by using clues in the sighter during a drift. Potential bites from a fish can cause the sighter to move, dip, stop, speed up, slow down, hesitate, or do nothing at all. This is where experience and intuition come into play.

Light and sensitive gear makes it more likely to feel when a fish takes the fly. However, if you feel the take, the fish also feels the resistance and can release the fly much faster. I often say that if you feel the bite, you are already too late. My goal is to always *see* the takes. When anglers tell me they feel all their bites but miss the fish, I quickly conclude that they could be fishing flies that are too heavy. Try switching to slightly lighter flies, to help detect the bite before you feel it. Detecting strikes takes time; to really get good at it takes a willing attitude to adjust.

During guide trips, I like to teach by counting bites during the fishing session. I get some strange looks from students when I tell them we will be counting bites and misses. Anglers seem to have a short-term memory when it comes to missed fish, or they do not want to admit it. Detecting bites is an art form; it takes time and can look slightly different in every run or situation. Use the missed fish as a learning tool to help you understand the bigger picture. I have often had students disagree with me when I say, "That's a bite!" I am not exactly sure why anglers want to hesitate or disagree about takes. It could be because they are not used to tiny movements in the sighter that are actually fish.

Euro nymphing techniques can open opportunities to detect more bites than even experienced fly anglers are used to. I often see anglers question and disbelieve that the incredibly small motion they saw in the sighter could be a bite. We have all heard someone on a video or podcast say hook sets are free—although they are not exactly "free," it is important to set often while euro nymphing. You will only learn what is or is not a bite if you set the hook.

Fish can eat and release the flies at lightning-fast speeds. If you are hesitant and slow on the hook set, you might not realize how many bites you are getting. I remember one of my students would not believe how many takes I said he was missing. He would hesitate, and the fish released the fly so quickly he would not feel anything as he set the hook. He did not think they were fish because he felt nothing. Instead, he rationalized that it was just the bottom. This is why we need to be hypervigilant and extremely focused.

During the winter months fish activity and metabolism can slow down, and the takes can be really soft. When this fish ate the fly, there was almost no indication in the sighter. A trained eye with lots of practice and a gut instinct prompted me to set the hook. ROCH MILLER

World Team USA member Sean Crocker is focused and concentrated on all aspects of his drift. His arms and hands are in a position to strike quickly as he intensely watches his sighter for any indication of a take.

The day slowly spiraled downward because he would question the takes, then hesitate even longer with every sighter movement, instead of just setting the hook. A trick we will learn about later, and one of the biggest points to me writing this book, is to fish lighter flies. Often lighter flies will hit the bottom less, or not at all, helping make the bites more obvious and easier to distinguish. Fishing a slower drift and encouraging fish to move up to eat the fly can also help to magnify the take.

The sighter can also show us how much tension our flies are under. If the sighter is straight, there is a tight connection to the flies. If the sighter is too loose, you might not be connected at all. The sighter helps us determine when to make important and proper adjustments. Reading how straight or sagged the sighter is during a drift will help us adjust our weight, tippet length, and rod angle. A setup with a heavier leader and sighter will naturally sag more than one with a lighter leader and sighter. If we want the flies to have less tension, we give the flies some slack. The lighter fly will not be as tight, showing up in the sighter with slightly more sag. That is usually what I am after, just the slightest amount of sighter sag, helping me see the takes and giving the fly just enough slack to help it move more freely during the drift.

Finding the sighter quickly after the cast can be difficult. A good cast helps set up a good sighter placement in the drift. I often watch anglers searching to find their sighter. Here is a good tip: Get to the point where you are not searching to find the sighter anymore. Identify your target on the water, make an accurate cast, and the sighter should reveal itself as it comes into sight. The sighter should find you; you are not looking for it. You should be in control during all aspects of your drift, knowing where your flies and sighter are at all times. Quickly seeing the sighter will also help indicate takes that happen at the beginning of the drift.

If you get tired, lose focus, and start making sloppy drifts, take a break. It can be beneficial to take a moment and refocus before making another cast. Sloppy drifts can sometimes just spook fish.

DRIFT SEQUENCE

Let us discuss more technical components of a drift as the flies travel through the water. This can help us understand what the flies are doing through the drift and better adjust. For example, the first part of the drift is where the flies enter the water and sink to depth. Then connection with the flies is obtained when we lift the rod tip as the flies travel downstream. The flies can be fished deep with a vertical angle to help the flies slow down as the leader slides under the rod tip. Then the flies come under more tension and start to swing at the tail end of the drift.

It is important to understand drift position and what the flies should be doing in that section. Also, if a fish eats during a specific part of the drift consistently, we can adjust our technique and body position to maximize that

Drift position photo. JOE CLARK

Drift Positions

Position 1: After the initial cast, the flies enter the water into position 1 and start to sink. To help maintain connection and encourage the flies to sink, floating the sighter could be helpful. It will help us detect a bite and allow the flies to sink at a slightly farther distance. If the goal is to keep the flies high in the column, start the drift immediately by leading the flies downstream or having a shallow rod angle. Fish that are actively eating close to the surface or in shallow water often eat the flies immediately after casting. Maintaining connection is important throughout position 1.

Position 2: Usually the sweet spot of the drift is around position 2. The flies are close to the bottom or hopefully to the desired depth. Line management can be important now, as you might need to slowly raise the rod tip or retrieve the line as the flies move downstream from position 1 to position 2. This will help maintain connection and manage incoming slack. Management will also help slow down the drift and control the depth. As you lift the leader from the water, gravity will cause the leader and sighter to naturally sag. The sag will also help keep the flies connected so we can detect bites. Many fish that I catch are in the drift from when the flies hit the water to near position 3. If a fish eats during that part of the drift, it means the fish is upstream of my body when I set the hook, resulting in a helpful downstream hook set. The fish will then be at the correct position to fight and bring downstream into the net.

Position 3: The flies are closest to our rod tip in position 3. The closer the leader and flies are under the rod tip, the more control we have over the drift. You can help achieve a deep drift or slow down the presentation by using a vertical rod and sighter angle from position 2 through position 3. That is one way we can really slow down the drift to crawl the flies close to the bottom.

Position 4: Position 4 is downstream from our body position. Extra tension is added to the drift as connection starts and the flies start to lift. The trick to slowing down the lifting of the flies is to lower the fly rod tip toward the water to create slack, which maintains the drift's depth longer. Try to keep the sighter at the same distance above the water as you lower the rod tip. There will be a point where you cannot go any farther downstream with the fly rod and the flies will naturally rise under the tension. Fish will often come as the flies turn from their deep, slow drift and begin to lift. The flies will then start to rise from

continued

the bottom to the surface at position 5. Position 4 is what we refer to as a downstream drift, like a Colorado drift. It can be an effective way to fish deep water, especially when you cannot get the right body position to fish the situation.

Position 5: This position is the end of the drift. It is where the flies cannot drift downstream any farther. Often the flies end near or at the surface of the water. Hanging the flies in the current for a second sometimes can result in a take. I have experienced times when fish are rising, especially in fast water. Getting the fly to hang over their position can work well. During the early season Grannom hatch, I will let my flies hang downstream when I see splashy random rises. The flies suspended in the water close to the surface are sometimes just irresistible to hungry trout. However, the farther the flies drift downstream, the harder it becomes to convert hook sets into landed fish.

part of the drift over the best water. For example, if fish are quickly taking the flies at the very beginning of the drift, this could mean the fish are high in the water column, highly active, or looking up. The beginning part can have less drag and be a more natural part of the drift. Watch at what point during the drift the fish are biting.

Learning from the Drift

A missed fish to most anglers is just a missed fish. For me, a missed fish is an opportunity to learn. Missing fish could be a good indicator that you may have picked a good play, or the right technique and approach. Every time a fish eats our passing offering is a chance for us to see more than just a bite or missed fish. Each bite can be analyzed to understand a lot about what is going on underneath the water.

A good competitor can figure out how to catch trout as quickly as possible during a fishing session. Sometimes that takes changing a fly or weight or presenting the flies with different techniques. Drifting flies can be done more than one way. There are many ways we can show fish our flies to tempt them to eat. I have a progression of techniques, from floating the sighter to jigging my flies, to help me figure out what will work.

A few years ago, during the spring in central Pennsylvania, I told my student that I was going to fish the stream for 30 minutes before our guide day to help hone the technique for that day. Each bite would give me a clue as to how the fish were eating. Also, I could analyze where the bite happened during the drift. If you had a bite and missed it, instead of casting back, take a minute to think. Did the bite happen at the beginning of the cast during the sink, or in

Both a missed and a captured fish provide data that can help anglers make appropriate adjustments. Where did the fish take during the drift, how hard was the take, and what could I have done better with my drift or approach? These are questions I like to think about while fishing to help me adjust my approach—not just for that day, but also for the next time I am in a comparable situation. DOMINIC LENTINI

US Youth team member Drew Bone anticipated the bite for this large fish when his nymph drifted through the best part of the run. Every time Drew approached the same water type—depth and speed—he would get a fish. He noted that data and could almost predict when the next fish would happen as we approached similar types of water on the next run. BRIAN KIMMEL

the middle when the flies were deep? The bite could even happen when the flies started to lift and swing at the tail end of the drift. Knowing at what point the fish bites in the drift can help us understand things like what depth to fish, how active and aggressive the fish are, and if our drift is what they want.

When we miss fish, even the way they take our fly can give us details we can use to adjust our approach. Was it a soft or aggressive take? Are the fish actively eating, or were the bites slow and soft? All this info can help us adjust our technique and how quickly we move through the water. It would take another book to explain all the tactics and ideas that I have gained from fishing. The point of adding this here is to encourage anglers to start keeping track of how and where the bite happened, and to keep data that will help in the future.

Taking it one step further, I recently talked to a former student who recalled a time when I was demonstrating my approach in a series of fast water pockets. He said something like, "I saw you catch fish without any indication in the sighter." He said it seemed like some sort of crazy fishing magic, but it was not. We call this anticipation. I am using data from fish that I previously missed or captured that day to help me better predict where bites happen during the drift.

CONTROL

The angler needs to be in the driver's seat to better control every drift, this takes focus and control. Euro nymphing is a short-range technique, but it is possible to fish slightly farther with good line control. We also need to learn how to control our drift and cast with smooth and deliberate movements. A shaky drift will create a bounce through the fly rod into the sighter that makes it tough to detect bites. Sometimes to catch the fish, it takes multiple moving parts and years of practice.

I recently fished a spring creek in Pennsylvania during one of the colder months of winter. I had a day where it seemed like the fish needed the drift to be precise. I could have caught a few without getting technical, but on that day, they needed the flies to pass by in a specific way and speed. It took a bit of trial and error to work through my techniques, covering enough good holding water to start catching numbers of fish.

It was not until I caught a few that I noticed trends to how they were biting, how aggressive the take was, and where I was finding them in the water. I used that data to help dial in my technique to present the flies to the fish how I thought they wanted them. In this case it was lighter flies cast at a slightly farther distance, with a deep-angled drift and extreme control. This was one of those times that it would have been difficult to instruct a brand-new student without some previous experience. Euro nymph fishing can be easy, but there are so many layers to discover and new things to learn. It can be very technical sometimes, so focus on creating a solid foundation with smooth control to help build your technique.

Accuracy, quick connection, and line control require a lot of practice. Fish do not always eat when we are ready; sometimes it happens the second the flies hit the water, and other times when we are not prepared. Control with our cast, rod angles, and line management will help us be more fluent while fishing. JOE CLARK

ROD MOVEMENTS

Every movement should be smooth and deliberate. A shaky hand will bounce the fly rod, putting vibrations in the sighter. I see seasoned anglers fishing with their arm fully extended all day. Ever try to hold your arm out all day? You get tired fast, and that makes for a shaky drift. The trick to a smooth drift is to keep your arm in close and elbow in line with your hand and shoulder. To take it a step further, the real trick for unsteady anglers is to lock the elbow of the arm holding the rod against your body. Instead of using the shoulders to move the fly rod downstream during the drift, turn at the hips. This will give you smooth and level movement throughout the entire drift. Gordon Vanderpool was the first to show me that trick.

To execute a good drift, the angler needs to complete a series of movements with their arm, wrist, shoulder, or all three. The goal is to glide the tip of the

rod with control downstream. Sometimes the rod will be raised—to control the slack or change the angle—during a drift. Sometimes the rod will need to glide in a straight line, parallel with the water. Smooth movements are so important to control the fly and to detect strikes. A shaky hand magnifies through the long rod, causing movement in the flies and sighter. We need to understand and master a smooth, controlled, and clean drift before we try to complicate it with more-technical nuances.

LINE MANAGEMENT AND SLACK RECOVERY

Farther distances and more-technical drifts depend on correctly managing line and recovering slack. Managing the line is important because bites can happen quickly and occur anywhere in the drift. It also helps us stay in connection with our flies and detect more strikes. Managing the line at first can

Limit excess and unnecessary movements like false casting while you fish. This will help improve overall efficiency, reduce unwanted tangles, and avoid spooking fish. JOE CLARK

Here I use the vector technique to contain slack as the nymphs drift downstream. It allows me to use a lower rod angle, which helps with control throughout the drift. JOE CLARK

be slightly difficult for some anglers, but the goal is for it to become second nature, using quick and smooth movements without looking down to keep focus on the sighter.

Slack can be controlled by lifting the fly rod during a drift. An elevated rod angle can put extra tension on the flies. Overhead trees or obstacles, however, can restrict us from elevating the fly rod too high. In those situations, the best way to control slack is to use a hand retrieve.

When an angler is fishing at a distance and not controlling their slack, they may try to manage slack by raising or elevating the fly rod tip high in the air. I have seen anglers with their rod nearly straight up in the air while trying to control their drift and slack. The first problem this creates is a terrible hook set angle. If the rod is already raised, there is little room to set the hook properly because the rod is so high.

The lower rod angle can help anglers set the hook faster. While guiding I like to use the analogy of a snake ready to bite. When my rod tip is elevated too high, there is no room for a strike. When my rod is low, I am in an advantageous position ready to strike.

Slack management is best controlled with the angler's line hand. There are a few different ways to manage line. The methods I feel are the best are a hand twist (like the figure 8 method that is popular when lake fishing) and the vector.

These methods use different hand movements to pull in line and control slack while drifting the flies. Remember, some slack is sometimes necessary to allow the flies to move more freely or sink quicker in the water. We need to be aware that balance is needed between being either too tight or not connected with too much slack. A good drift can depend on good line management.

Figure 8/Hand Twist

A good line management technique is called the figure 8/hand twist. It requires the angler to use their line hand in a twisting motion that will draw in line as the drift moves toward them. Weaving the leader between your fingers, you can pull in line smoothly. I remember learning about figure 8 fishing in lake competitions. It is a common retrieve used by lake

Line management with a figure 8/hand twist is crucial while euro nymph fishing. Here Josh uses his line hand to manage extra slack during the drift. You can also see that the part of the leader he is managing is thicker than the fishing part of the leader. Using a slightly thicker-diameter handling section makes it easier to grab or feel to control the line. RODGER OBLEY

and river anglers when fishing nymphs and streamers. Sean Crocker taught me how important the figure 8 is while retrieving my flies during a competition in north Georgia.

One problem you might encounter with the figure 8 is that it tends to slowly coil and kink a section of the leader. It will also over time cause the leader to stretch and coil and could cause the line to wrap around the butt of the fly rod or the reel. It can even create a breaking spot, especially when fishing with thin-diameter leaders.

Even with these potential problems, I like using the hand twist. The angler can keep their hands close to the reel while managing slack. It is important to have both hands close together to enable a quick reaction and the most possible control for when a fish takes the flies. If your hands are too far away, there can be a disconnect or slack created when trying to regain control of the line.

Vector

The vector line management technique is a simple trick that helps retrieve a good bit of line quickly and smoothly. I use the vector method most often when fishing fast water because of the need to pick up or manage a lot of line quickly. Holding the fly rod, make sure the leader is captured under a finger on the hand holding the handle of the fly rod—what I call the trigger finger. For a vector, the drag of the fly reel needs to be fairly tight so the line does not come off the reel. Make the shape of a V with the thumb and index finger of your line hand. Use the groove in the webbing of your thumb to hold the leader right where it comes out of the fly reel.

The trick is, just like a pulley system, there should be one fixed point, and that is from the reel. The two pulleys would then be both hands. Starting with your hands together, as you pull the line it should slide through the V in your line hand. Move that hand away from the rod to your side. Line should also slide under the part of the line that is captured under your finger on the rod hand.

Whatever the amount of line you pull as your vector, it is doubling the amount of line. It is like what I learned in grade school: When you try to lift something heavy, a movable pulley can help reduce the weight. The concept is the same here but obviously used in a unique way. So, I can use my entire wingspan, with my arms stretched wide, to pull lots of slack. My wingspan is just over 5 feet, but using the vector I am pulling in over 10 feet of line. Try to do this with one long, smooth movement.

I discovered the vector method while at a Team USA Youth clinic in western North Carolina. Gordon Vanderpool, Josh Stevens, and Paul Bourcq were teaching a group on the river advanced euro nymphing techniques. They were talking about managing a lot of slack quickly to stay connected to their flies at a farther distance. Paul demonstrated how fast he could retrieve a bunch of line using smooth movements to not interfere with the drift.

SPEED

I have found that the speed of the drift is one of the most key factors of euro nymphing. One rule to remember is that the speed of the water on the surface of the stream is faster than the water on or near the bottom. Water is a crazy thing; sometimes subsurface water is moving quickly and other times almost not moving at all. Sometimes it is hard to know what is going on underneath the surface. Using a euro nymphing approach and techniques like different rod angles, thinner tippet, and thin-profile flies will help reduce drag. This can help slow down the fly under the surface for a more natural drift. Weight can be helpful to slow down the drift, but practiced anglers can also slow the fly with their technique.

I am focused not only on the drift, but also on obtaining different drift speeds past the fish, trying to figure out what they want. Sometimes it is trial and error. For example, an angler might cast 10 times with a medium-angle drift and not catch fish, causing them to rethink their fly pattern when all it might take is slowing down the fly with a different rod angle.

In shallow pockets, flies can quickly end up on the bottom. Often my goal is to slow down the fly as much as possible without hitting the bottom. This is when I use a quarter cast and stop the rod high. Use a single nymph and hold the sighter higher off the water, fishing just enough tippet to get the flies near the bottom. JOE CLARK

"Time in the pocket" is a concept I use to help teach my students how to slow down the drift while euro nymphing, explaining that slowing down the drift sometimes is all it takes. I stand next to my client and have them cast upstream. We then count aloud how many seconds their drift lasts from start to finish. I make the same cast but manipulate my technique to slow down the fly's speed as much as possible. I demonstrate to show the students how much slower I can get my drift without changing the actual setup, merely by manipulating my technique with rod angles.

The trick of counting the seconds helps determine how much slower the flies are moving and how much time the flies are in the water. The longer your flies are in the water, the greater your chances of catching more fish. Speed can teach us a lot about fish, and that will help you develop a fishing instinct.

LIGHTER FLIES

I have learned so many new concepts, techniques, and fishing approaches while traveling, coaching, and competing. My success has come from figuring some things out on my own, coupled with always trying to seek knowledge from more-experienced anglers. I have been fortunate to learn from some of the best anglers in the world. After years of practice and adjustments, I have found myself repeatedly coming back to the use of lighter-weight flies.

I have noticed that some newer anglers gravitate toward using heavier flies. It is because flies with more weight help move the leader and cast the flies. Heavier flies are also easier for the angler to "feel" and control during the cast and drift. The downfall with heavy flies is they can limit natural movement during a drift.

Lighter flies can move more naturally in the water but are slightly harder to control and cast. It is also much harder to "feel" the flies during the drift. Here are two things I think might surprise anglers: how fast small flies will sink, and the fact that the flies do not always need to get to the bottom.

The thought of *constantly* ticking or hitting bottom is an idea we need to move away from. Not only could we be fishing underneath the fish, but ticking bottom makes it harder to determine whether you have a bite or just the next rock. My goal is to get the flies *near* the bottom—and to slow down. I

Pro Tip

Perdigon flies sink much faster than common nymphs, which is a big advantage especially in deep, fast water. You can afford to use smaller bead sizes with Perdigon Nymphs. —David Chlumsky was taught that ticking bottom was necessary while nymph fishing, and using indicators and split shot and ticking bottom *did* produce fish. However, euro nymphing is different in that the fly *is* the weight.

If the flies are hitting bottom, it is extremely hard to determine if there is a bite. If the sighter is constantly bouncing and moving, it is tough to see the softest bites. This could be one reason some bites can be *extremely* soft and hard to identify. When flies are fished in the water column or slightly above the fish, the bite is much easier to detect. When your flies are not touching bottom often, any sighter movement has a greater chance to be a fish. This is a big learning opportunity as you practice that will allow you to experience how soft and subtle some bites are.

Tricks to Get Light Flies Deep

Just because you are fishing a larger river does not mean you need to use heavy flies. In streams covered in whitewater, or in dirty water, anglers gravitate to this thought. Heavy flies sometimes could be the answer, but first I try to use slightly lighter flies and adjust my approach.

I have learned to use specialized gear and techniques that help with adjusting the cast and approach before physically changing the setup. One way to help get light flies deeper is to cast farther upstream. More distance between where you cast into the water and where you start the drift gives the flies time to sink. As the flies drift back toward the rod tip, they will continue to sink to depth. The farther you cast upstream, the more time the flies will have to sink.

Controlled slack will also help flies sink to depth. Tension on the flies slows down sink rate. Giving the flies some slack will help the flies sink much quicker to depth. Partnered with slack, a trick to get light flies to sink at various levels and help us control our depth is time. I use a counting system to help control how deep I will fish the drift.

Cast toward your target. After the cast, immediately lower the rod tip near the water. This will help produce the slack needed to help sink the fly. Count one while watching the sighter as it drifts downstream. Be aware that fish often eat the flies as they sink because they are sinking more naturally without tension. We call this "fishing the fall." The slack will let flies sink freely. After one second, come into direct contact by raising the fly rod to bring the leader and sighter above the water. Next, repeat the steps. Cast and stop the fly rod, then drop the rod tip and promote slack. Float the sighter for two seconds. The flies will now be even deeper on this drift. Raise the rod to recover the connection. The longer the flies have slack, the more quickly the flies will sink. So for each second you gain more depth. This method gives an angler the ability to fish various levels of the water column without changing the weight of the flies. This trick is especially good when fishing slightly lighter-weighted flies. It gives us more flexibility to change drifts and get the flies to fish at different levels in the water.

The tuck cast is another effective way to get flies deeper because it can *force* the flies into the water. A tuck cast can be performed on most casts in conjunction with techniques like the counting method. All these techniques rely on having good control and connection to detect bites.

Thinner tippet will also help get light flies to descend faster through the water. Thinner line will be affected less by drag as the current pushes against the line downstream. The thinner the tippet, the less drag against the line and the slower we can get the drift. It is important to understand there is a limit to how thin the tippet should be. First and most important, we never want to over-fight and exhaust fish. Over-fighting can injure the fish, and we also do not want to lose more flies.

Revisiting fly profiles from Chapter 4, remember that thin flies help cut through the water easier and with less drag. Flies like a Perdigon and France boast a very slim profile. Their slim shape creates less drag against the fly as it sinks to the bottom. You can rely on those flies to sink quicker than the same weighted fly that has a much bulkier profile.

TIPPET MEASUREMENT

I like to think that fly fishing in a way is mathematical, but when you add the wild card of a living fish, that can change any outcome. Euro nymph fly fishing has many variables that produce many different outcomes. My goal is to be able to control as many variables as possible and turn them into constants. For example, only having a few confidence flies to choose from allows the angler to change their mindset from finding the correct pattern to refining their drifts. This forces us to focus on other variables, like reading water, making better drifts, or when to change our setup. With euro nymphing there are a few variables we can adjust that will result in the flies drifting in different ways. We can change our rod angle or adjust the weight of our flies to get the flies to slow down or speed up.

Anglers often ask me how much tippet they should be using underneath their sighter. As with anything with euro nymphing, it is not always a cut-and-dried answer. Tippet length is an important variable that can change our drift and the way flies are presented to the fish.

The length of the tippet you are using needs to be able to change depending on the approach, technique, and weight of your flies. The use of longer tippet in the water will increase slack. Slack can give the flies the ability to move freely while drifting. However, slack using lengthy tippet can easily create a disconnect to the flies.

Yet, using a short section of tippet could restrict the flies' movement during a drift. Fishing with short tippet tightly connected with the flies can result in quickly feeling takes and missing the bite. Techniques like floating the sighter can benefit from longer lengths of tippet to help keep the flies from hitting the

Take the time to measure your tippet each time you add a new piece to the leader. Consistency will help you learn and re-create what has worked in the past. DOMINIC LENTINI

bottom as fast. Instead of fishing a single fly with a directly connected technique in shallow pocketwater, I will use a much shorter tippet.

Knowing your measurements, especially tippet length, can help you better understand the drift and what the flies are doing. Anytime I add a new piece of tippet to the setup, I make sure to accurately measure each piece. This trick is helpful when I break off a fish and can easily replicate the setup with the exact amount of tippet I was just using.

I found that fishing the same tippet length helped me understand drifts and weight adjustments a little more in depth. I know that there is a difference in weight between a 2.5 mm and 2.8 mm fly, but sometimes it is hard to tell. When you fish the same tippet length over and over, that small difference in weight is much more obvious.

My trick to tippet measurements is using the length of my arms. I will hold the spool with one hand and stretch the tippet. My first measurement with my arms outstretched is from my hand to my armpit. The second measurement point would be to the other armpit. The last would be my full wingspan. This gives me a few different lengths but has consistency when changing the tippet.

During times when I decide it is appropriate to use a two-fly setup, I will use one arm's length from my hand, holding the spool to my armpit. This ensures that my flies will be spaced apart properly, approximately 20 inches. Consistency is important, as is controlling as many variables as you can while euro nymphing.

THE DRIFTS

Shallow, Medium, and Deep Rod Angles (SMD)

Having versatility with our drift when nymph fishing is important for a quick and effective way to cover different types of water or change the way the flies move. Fish can be positioned throughout the water column at various times. They can be close to flat on the bottom, suspended mid-column, or even right under the surface. When anglers think of nymphing, there seems to be an assumption that the flies need to go straight and be fished right at the bottom. You will often hear anglers say, "You always need to be ticking bottom to catch fish." I have learned that this is far from the truth. The temperature and available food will often draw fish to sit higher off the bottom, so fishing deep is not always the answer.

The technique we call shallow, medium, and deep (SMD) will help us be more versatile and cover more depths of water. This method also can give the flies a separate way to drift past the fish. We could adjust the tippet length or change weights of the flies, but that takes time. Instead of physically changing the setup, we can adjust the rod and the sighter angle with the SMD technique to help control the depth of the flies. Let us talk about why fish sit in different columns of water.

Seasoned angler Nick Meloy knows the importance of making quick adjustments to his drift by manipulating his rod angles. After spotting this fish in clear water, he adjusted the angle of his rod and leader to help slow down the speed of the fly to entice this beautiful brown trout. BRITTANY FUNCHEON

Rainbow trout can oftentimes be suspended midway or even higher up in the column of water. They can even be actively swimming around and looking for food. Brown trout, however, especially our Pennsylvania wild brown trout, tend to stay closer to the bottom. But any species of trout that is sitting near the bottom could quickly suspend mid-column or right below the surface waiting for food.

Hatches move fish from resting places to eating lanes. Temperature can be the deciding factor for a fish's metabolism or for kick-starting a hatch to get fish to suspend in the column. A quick cold front could push the fish right to near the bottom. However, the start of a hatch could draw them back. Changes in conditions and where fish will sit can happen quickly, so it is important to have an adjustable technique with the drift to fish changing conditions.

Fish often look straight ahead and above in the water. If you are fishing rainbows and your fly is on the bottom, potentially below the fish, the fish might never see the fly. Partially for this reason, I like to start my first drifts higher in the water column when fishing in deeper water. It will ensure the flies cover fish that could be suspended before I fish closer to the bottom.

SMD gives us the ability to quickly adjust depth and the way the flies drift with each cast. The use of long fly rods and leaders opens potential adjustments we can make to our approach and technique to effectively fish more conditions we encounter. SMD is best performed by using different angles of the fly rod, leader, and sighter. Without changing our setup, we can manipulate rod angles to let the flies sink fast or hold them from sinking as quickly.

When fishing moving water there are so many different depths and speeds, and not all spots are the same. The most common adjustments we make to our setup to properly fish at different depths is first to adjust weight and tippet length. Luckily, SMD gives us ways to control the angle of the drift by adjusting the rod, which can help increase or decrease sink rate for the flies.

I witnessed this technique while coaching my first US Youth clinic in North Carolina. Coaches of the US Youth team, Gordon Vanderpool and Paul Bourcq, were standing in the middle of the river explaining the importance of versatility. As a competitive angler, managing time is crucial because you are racing against the clock. We are often placed into a stream or waters that we have never fished before. It is important to have a technique that can cover various water types and depths without having to change the fly or our setup—like an all-purpose play. Fly changes take time, and time is precious when competing. Gordon and Paul taught the group the importance of having a technique that can be versatile to cover lots of different water depths and types. A clever way to describe the technique is with the term "sighter angles."

A "shallow-angled" drift can help anglers keep the flies higher in the water column. It is a good technique for fishing in shallow water because it will help keep the flies from quickly sticking on the bottom. It can be difficult to fish in water that is less than 1 foot, especially at greater distances, because even lightly weighted flies will still quickly end up on the bottom with a vertical rod angle, unless you hold the flies off the bottom. A shallow rod angle will help encourage the flies to sit higher in the water to make a drift. A rod might only be 1 to 3 feet above the water, keeping the leader and sighter at a low and shallow angle to the flies. The leader from the tip of the fly rod should be at a shallow angle, almost perpendicular to the surface of the water. This low and shallow angle will maintain itself under the water toward the flies, keeping them higher in the water column. Gravity will push downward on the leader and sighter, causing it to sag or "belly." The sag will create some tension on the flies. The tension will help keep the flies connected with the sighter and rod tip and encourage them to move downstream slightly faster to help avoid the bottom.

The Frisbee cast helps put you in position to fish a shallow angle. Stop the fly rod early, which helps make a quick connection. Immediately start to lead the flies downstream at the same speed as the surface water with the rod tip low, keeping everything in a straight line and connected. Maintaining a low rod angle as the flies drift downstream will help keep the flies connected and higher in the water column. Oftentimes, because of the extra tension and connection with the flies, you will feel the strike. It is also important to experiment with your speed.

A shallow angle can also be a good approach or starting point when fishing in deeper water. It is used to keep the flies closer to the surface in case fish are

Joe Clark fishes with a low rod and sighter angle to help keep the flies from hanging up on the bottom.

Pro Tip

Do not fish like a robot. Constantly change your technique to adapt to different water conditions. Don't try to force one technique to work on an entire river. Be flexible and make changes to your fly weight and rod angles to adjust to the water you are fishing. —Sean Crocker

suspended up in the water. In this case I will use a shallow-angled drift to keep the flies closer to the surface. Any angle change, including the shallow angle, will present the flies in a different way than other drifts, giving the flies a different look to the fish. It is important to be diversified and show fish the flies in various ways.

Another play is the "medium angle." Like a shallow angle, it will give the flies a different drift and depth. Elevating the rod slightly higher will let the flies sink more to depth. This drift is around a 45 percent angle in the leader. Although I will rotate between all three angles, the medium angle is a good balance between sag, tension, and drag.

The third play I will touch on is a "vertical" or almost vertical drift. It will help slow down the flies even more. It can be harder to stay in connection

Joe Clark slows down his presentation by elevating his fly rod as the leader starts to move, creating a medium-angled drift. A slight sag in the sighter can help identify takes. JOSH MILLER

Joe Clark slows down his drift by elevating the rod to get a deep-angle drift. JOSH MILLER

when fishing a deep-angled drift if you are using long tippet. Lots of tippet can create a disconnect to the flies, resulting in missing the takes, especially when using light flies. The sighter helps us control the depth. Raise the sighter higher off the water using the technique we call "fishing the flies." I like to picture my flies directly connected in a straight line through my sighter to the rod tip. Having extra tippet under the water will create a bow and could pull the flies downstream quicker. Try to keep your rod tip slightly downstream of the sighter while drifting.

FISHING THE FLIES AND FISHING THE SIGHTER

Fishing the sighter and fishing the flies are two different concepts. Fishing the sighter is when an angler has the end sighter just off the surface of the water. The problem with this is the angler might have too much tippet under the water, not knowing what the flies are doing. The target depth and where the fish could be holding are constantly changing. Every spot we fish varies in depth and speed. However, fishing the flies is a way to manipulate how we fish our flies depending on how deep we want them to be in the water, without changing the setup. The sighter is what we use as our point of reference to determine how deep the flies are. We want to always be in control and know where our flies are throughout the drift. This technique is another reason euro nymphing is so versatile.

At the start of each fishing day, I string up the fly rod and add a piece of tippet below the sighter. I will add a section of tippet that is average to the water depth I will be fishing. It is not the perfect measurement because each fishing spot is different. It would be annoying and take so much time if I had to change tippet length for varying depths.

Fishing the sighter is how most euro anglers start out fishing, without knowing it. It is how I learned to euro nymph fish. We at times want to fish just enough tippet to get the flies near the bottom without extra slack. The problem is fishing the same amount of tippet every time you drift in shallow or deeper water. Oftentimes I will see anglers fishing their sighter really close to the water, thinking they are helping their flies slow down more or get even deeper. My goal is to have the fly just off the bottom. Imagine a scenario where the fly is just off the bottom in water that is around 2 feet deep. Let us say the tippet length from the end of the sighter to the bottom fly is 4 feet. If the angler is fishing the sighter with the sighter close to the water, there will be an extra 2 feet of tippet under the water. I envision the tippet now connecting with the fly underwater in the shape of an L or a big underwater bow. This will cause the fly to have extra drag and make it harder to slow down the drift.

A better way to fish water that is 2 feet deep with 4 feet of tippet is to fish the flies by raising the sighter. The sighter is lifted above the water 2 feet to take up the extra tippet length. The flies are fished just off the bottom with a

Nick Yardley makes an adjustment when he moves into a section of river that is much shallower. He holds his sighter high off the water to adjust for the shallow depth without having to shorten his tippet for when he moves upstream back to deeper water. DOMINIC LENTINI

Euro nymphing is a versatile technique that gives anglers the ability to adjust on the go. Raise the sighter higher off the water to drift the flies in shallower water. DOMINIC LENTINI

controlled, directly connected drift. The best way for me to describe this to my students is that we are acting like a suspension device. We are holding and suspending the setup from hitting the bottom.

The concept of fishing the flies gives the angler a good technique and approach to fishing more depths of water without having to change their setup. I picture my flies underwater in a straight line from where my tippet enters the water to the flies slightly upstream. My anchor or point fly is suspended just off the bottom. The tag fly will be in a straight line above the anchor fly, then the tippet will continue in a straight line up to the water surface to the sighter. Slightly leading the flies downstream will ensure connection with the flies and indicate through the sighter when anything encounters the flies.

Don't Sink the Sighter

Although anglers feel the urge to sink the sighter during a drift, try not to. If you sink the sighter during a drift, the thicker-diameter line will catch more current and cause more drag. The flies will be pushed downstream slightly faster, hindering the drift.

Sighter material when drifted under the water can also spook fish. I have seen fish in low, clear water spook even at the glimpse of sighter material floating on the surface. Anglers often fish part of the sighter underwater in hopes of forcing a fly deeper. It might speed up the drift. It is also harder to "read" the sighter if it is submerged under the surface, especially because my eyes are always focused on the bottom end of the sighter.

If you are fishing water that is exceptionally varied in depth and do not want to constantly change the setup, fish with a thinner sighter, close to the tippet size you are using. If the water is very deep, sinking a thin piece of sighter will not spook the fish all the way at the bottom, and it will let you drift without having to switch the tippet length.

Instead of sinking the sighter, the colored sighter wax we discussed in Chapter 2 can come in handy. A sighter can be painted onto the line and quickly changed and adjusted by wiping it off. I am sure there are times that I will sink the sighter under the water in one of those deep holes, but I try to adjust my tippet length instead of fishing the sighter underwater too often.

One Hand Trick

Have you ever learned that it is important to build something with a solid foundation? While euro nymphing is simple, there are some technical and moving components to some drifts. For instance, fishing at a farther distance is good, but when fished with poor technique it will only hinder your drifts. Gordon Vanderpool and I were teaching a class in Colorado. I made a few drifts without catching a fish. He grabbed my rod, made two consecutive drifts, and caught two fish. He quickly pointed out that I was fishing slightly too far away. The distance I was fishing did not allow me to slow down and control the drift as to how the fish wanted it.

Joe Clark demonstrates fishing at close range with one hand in this shallow pocket. It is good to build more advanced and technical drifts at farther distances after you have polished more basic techniques. JOSH MILLER

A good drift at a farther distance takes control and a good base technique, and sometimes isn't necessary. All anglers need to master simple techniques before trying to fish more of a technical approach. In other words, master the short game of euro nymphing before trying to fish farther distances. Euro nymphing at a distance can be super effective and can help you spook fewer fish and cover more fish with longer drifts.

While guiding and teaching euro nymphing, anglers tend to pull out too much line from the fly reel and try to fish way too far away. Fishing at farther distances can be the goal and will absolutely lead to more fish over time. Start off simple and close and practice building good technique. New students would benefit from fishing at closer distances without focusing on extra aspects. With practice you will get better at fishing farther distances. It takes hours on the water to achieve line control.

Fishing at a distance requires the angler to manage multiple aspects to maintain connection and get a good drift. Removing the extra aspects of the drift and stripping it down to the basics will help anglers achieve good drifts, a better understanding of the cast, and a quick connection with the flies. A way to help simplify euro nymphing is to only fish with one hand. Put your non-dominant hand behind your back, making it difficult to fish far away. This will eliminate the extra variables, like line management and slack recovery, to help you focus solely on the rod hand making good drifts.

FLOAT THE SIGHTER

Floating the sighter can be difficult for the seasoned euro angler who is used to keeping tightly connected to the flies. Floating the sighter was my first go-to method to fish shallow water with light nymphs. The technique is productive in fast, deep water as well. The method allows the flies to move freely in the water while still maintaining connection through the leader and sighter. Floating the sighter can be done with any euro leader and can be integrated into any drift to help fish farther distances.

The goal while floating the sighter is to have the leader and sighter material sit on the surface of the water. You need to be able to see the strikes. Sighter materials built from Amnesia float well and are highly visible. Thicker diameters will also float higher and longer.

There are ways to build leaders designed specifically for this method. You may find that many of these leaders are heavier for floating. Lighter leaders will work with this technique but are harder to see and will not stay afloat as long.

When floating the sighter, it is important to fish the flies, leader, and sighter all in the same current seam and at the same speed. If the flies land in water moving faster than the sighter, there is a disconnect to the flies, resulting in missing or not even detecting the takes. To compensate for this, pulling the leader and flies downstream for a short distance will help get everything into

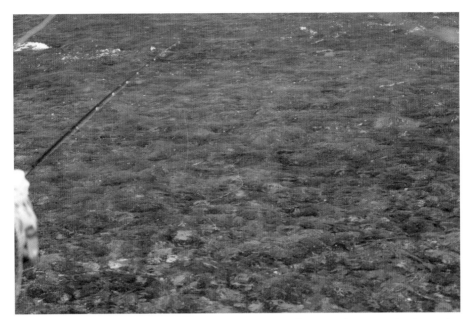

While floating the sighter, the entire length of the sighter does not always need to be on the water. In various water speeds, you can better control the drift by lifting different lengths of sighter from the water. JOSH MILLER

the same current lane. There are tricks to casting to manipulate the leader so it will land in the same current line, like a reach cast.

Floating the sighter is also a multipurpose technique. We can fish different depths of water without changing our weight by adjusting the cast. A cast that is connected immediately through the leader, sighter, and fly will restrict sink time and help you fish flies higher in the water column. A slight tuck cast or casting with some slack between the sighter and where the flies land in the water will give the flies time to sink. The current will then pull the leader and sighter downstream to regain connection with the flies. Greater depth and a slower drift can be accomplished with controlled slack, tippet length, and a tuck cast.

We need to be aware of our tippet length. There are times when using both long and short tippet is necessary. When fishing small streams, skinny water, or small pockets, I will fish a shorter amount of tippet to help get a more precise drift. However, when you use short tippet, the drift could end prematurely because the flies are likely to hit the bottom, which gives us what we call false bites. The sighter will jump when the flies hit the bottom, making it hard to distinguish a take. Longer tippet can help minimize false bites. Longer tippet also will encourage the sighter to stay on the surface, helping lengthen the drift. Longer tippet is harder to stay in connection with, especially with alternating current and water that is very broken. Both a single- or double-nymph setup can be productive while floating the sighter.

Floating the sighter helps me to fish lightweight flies farther upstream to the spooky fish in this slow water. RODGER OBLEY

World angler Pat Weiss meticulously covers all the fishy-looking holding spots while working the water. Here he starts with the closest water to where he entered the stream. Pat accurately casts underneath the near tree while floating the sighter looking for his next fish. JOSH MILLER

When fishing this method, it is beneficial to use wax to help the leader float. The wax will hold the line and leader on the surface of the water. A high floating leader is important as it will help you detect bites. The wax should be applied from the fly line, through the entire leader and sighter, to the connection of the tippet. A few extra knots in the leader and sighter can help hold extra wax and give the angler a visual reference.

If the sighter is too small, like 4X to 5X, it will limit the length of each drift. Thicker sighter like 0X to 3X will float longer than the thin tippet. In some situations, however, fish will spook as the thicker-colored sighter floats on the surface.

LEAD THE FLIES

Maintaining connection with the flies through the tippet and into the sighter is crucial to see the bites. Sometimes it is easy to stay in connection. But it can be difficult to understand what the current is doing. Turbulent and fast underwater currents will disconnect us from the flies. Flies often sweep under the sighter and get caught at different current speeds, which will result in a disconnection with the flies and consequently nothing to indicate a bite.

To lead the flies, move the rod downstream in the direction the flies will travel during the drift. This will keep connection with the fly rod through the leader to the flies. Moving the rod downstream with the current helps keep the flies upstream of the rod tip and in the same water seam or lane. When the flies swing too far under the rod tip, it is easy to lose connection; this is when you would speed up how fast you move the rod tip downstream. If you see slack or the sighter goes loose, move the rod tip downstream until the connection is regained, then slow back down.

Trout sometimes can be stacked in places that are difficult to drift, such as at the top of a run where the surface speed of the water can be moving very quickly. Fish like to congregate in this water type for several reasons. When anglers see fast water, their initial thought is to add more weight. Instead, let us first try to manipulate our approach and get lighter flies to the fish. During the cast, try leading the rod downstream before the fly even hits the water. Use the Frisbee cast and maintain a low angle while casting.

While fishing turbulent water that is broken into various speeds by underwater rocks, it can be easy to lose connection with the flies—especially when the flies are lightweight. Pops makes sure to sometimes lead his flies to ensure connection while fishing in broken water.
JOSH MILLER

Sometimes during a drift I notice the sighter will start to sag or turn downstream. The speed of the water underneath the surface can be much faster than we anticipate. Try lightly leading the flies downstream to regain connection, then slow back down. SARAH MILLER

With a small and controlled casting motion, cast the fly rod tip in a straight line toward the target. Make sure to stop the rod early to set up the rod position to start the drift. Stopping the rod early will help keep the flies directly upstream of the fly rod, in the same current seam as directly under the fly rod. The flies, leader, and rod tip should be tracking in the same current lane. It will help slow down the drift and interfere less with other current speeds. I commonly witness anglers trying to get the most distance out of their cast by following through too far forward, with the fly rod dropping the flies into another current lane. As the flies cast through the air toward the target, start moving the rod tip downstream about the same speed as the surface current. The rod should be already moving downstream as the flies are still in the air moving toward the water.

The sighter should be about a medium-angled drift and fly directly upstream of the fly rod's tip. The flies will sink through the faster water that is near the surface down to the slower water near the bottom. Then the flies will start to

I love fishing in shallow water—water depth that is between ankle and knee to be exact. Here I lead the flies with a low rod angle to help keep them from hanging up on the bottom in this very shallow run. RODGER OBLEY

"stick" in the slower underwater current, putting the brakes on the drift. This will alert the angler to slow down the drift, giving the fish time to see the flies.

If you find yourself having a challenging time slowing down your drift, first try adding the tuck cast. If necessary, change to a thinner tippet or switch to a slightly heavier-weighted fly. I always change the bottom fly weight first before changing the tag fly when fishing two flies. Having a heavier bottom fly should help keep the flies tracking better to maintain connection.

Taking it a bit further, when fish are eating quickly, heavily leading the flies can set up for a quick hook set. Last season during early summer, Joe and I were fishing upstream through a shallow, skinny stretch of water on a spring creek. The bites were so lightning fast, it was almost daunting. I remember missing a ridiculous number of fish before landing my first. One way I figured out to overcome the fast takes was to give the fish more slack to encourage them to hold the fly longer. The other method I used was to lead the flies heavily. The motion of leading the flies is already locked and loaded for a quick hook set, already "pulling" the flies and in direct connection, so there is nearly zero delay between when the fish eat and when you feel the take. Leading the flies is an important part of connection and should be in a well-rounded bag of euro nymphing tricks.

Creating movement to the fly can sometimes be all it takes to get a fish to take. Tom Emmons fooled this big brown trout while jigging his fly around some large boulders in deep pocketwater. TIM KRANICK

JIGGING FLIES

Jigging flies or adding extra movement and motion is an effective way to catch fish when bugs are active or fish are difficult. The bouncing motion of the flies moving up and down in the water during a drift can be enough to interest active or wary fish. The technique is especially productive when bugs are active. Bugs like caddis can swim aggressively toward the surface to hatch. When anglers give movement to their flies by jigging, it can look like the caddis moving toward the surface.

An effective time to jig your flies is after you have already finished a holding spot. Just the simple movement of a slightly jigged fly can help anglers pull one more fish. It is the vibrations the fly gives off, or the potential of food getting away. I experienced this fishing dirty water in one of my Team USA regional competitions. In practice, I discovered that jigging a single Walt's Worm in shallow pockets on the edge of the river was very productive. I looked over my section of stream, trying to identify all the similar water types that had been working in practice. In those spots I would jig the fly with regular success.

The best way to give movement to the flies is to bounce the fly rod. The jigging motion can be done by holding the fly rod with your pointer finger over the cork onto the fly rod's blank. Using your pointer finger, gently tap the rod. The tapping will slightly bounce the tip of the rod, sending a pulsing motion down to the flies. Try tapping the rod every second or half second. Another way to jig the flies is to slightly lift your wrist. The motion is very slight, just enough to bounce the flies.

I cast upstream, let the flies sink, and then come almost vertical with my sighter. I want to be directly connected at a deep-angled drift. After my flies have settled under my rod tip, I start to give motion to my flies by slightly bouncing my wrist. A trick that I found works is to jig each movement to the tempo of the Bee Gees song "Stayin' Alive."

This method works crazy good while euro nymph fishing with a dry-dropper setup—a heavy nymph underneath the dry fly and a caddis fly on the surface. The angler can lift the dry fly out of the water and the heavy nymph will quickly pull the dry fly back to the surface. Oftentimes fish cannot resist the motion of the dry fly dabbing on the surface.

FISHING A BELLY

Manageable sag is what we call "fishing a belly" in the sighter. It is not that sag is necessarily bad. We just need to learn the right amount through practice and instinct. The downward sag can help us stay in connection better with the flies. Turbulent water or varied water speeds can easily create a disconnect between the flies and the sighter. There are many ways to create sag. A heavier sighter and leader sag more, causing more pull on the flies but potentially pulling the flies through the drift, making the movement unnatural. Heavier flies can be used to help overcome the pull of the heavy leader. I like to try to fish lighter flies and lighter leaders with less sag, but there is a balance.

Thin leaders can have too much direct connection, and being tightly connected to the flies causes extra tension, so a little sag can help by allowing the fly to move in the water more freely. In that situation the angler could slightly decrease tension by switching to a lighter-weight fly, lengthening their tippet, or using a slightly heavier leader or sighter.

I focus on the water upstream while fishing a little sag, or belly in my sighter. ROGER OBLEY

Fishing a belly in the sighter can help anglers see when fish eat their flies. The belly could jump or move, magnifying the take. One trick to help encourage belly in the sighter is to use two different sizes of sighter. For instance, I will use 18 inches of 4X sighter and attach it to 18 inches of 4.5X sighter. Having a knot in the middle of the entire length of sighter will create a slight hinge and is a good focal point to help detect subtle strikes.

When fishing a setup without sag, anglers often will feel the bite sooner than they will see the take, missing the fish. In my experience, I would rather see the bite than feel the take; that gives me a second to respond. Fish hold the fly longer if there is slack and will not feel the resistance of the angler. Times when I was tightly connected to my flies I would often see the flash of the fish under the water as I felt the bite. For about a second I would have the fish on the line, then it would come off. Fishing with slightly lighter flies would be my first adjustment to create a small amount of slack in my leader. It is crazy, but sometimes all it takes is the slightest sag or "looseness" to get and convert more bites.

Having some sag in the leader will also give the fly slack, which gives the fly some "softness," allowing it to move more freely in the water. This is a term we heard while practicing for Youth Worlds in Poland. The river was wide and shallow, and the fish were spooky. A little bit of slack lets the fly naturally move in the water current. Rocks and uneven substrate in the river can create underwater micro currents that will push food, and not just downstream. Fish can be very aware of how bugs and debris move through the underwater current. While fishing, giving the fly a bit of slack will help the fly undulate more freely in the micro currents.

Another way to create sag is to fish heavier tippet. This will slow down the sink rate of the flies, creating slightly more slack. Oftentimes when using thin tippet, the flies end up sinking quickly through the current and getting stuck on the bottom. Increasing tippet size will slow the sink rate of the fly, but the thicker-diameter line will have a harder time slowing down.

SNAGS

Since nymph fishing is done subsurface, we tend to snag more and lose flies. This can be costly. Rocks, submerged wood, and structure have taken more flies from me than I can count. I have been frustrated by losing so many flies

Next time you get a snag, fight the urge to just keep pulling. Here I try to pull the flies out the opposite way they entered the snag. RODGER OBLEY

to the bottom that I have mastered the art of removing flies from underwater snags—which is also a technique.

I distinctly hear the voice of legendary angler Joe Humphreys saying, "You gotta risk it." Joe and I were fishing a small brushy stream in central Colorado, and he was pushing me to cast in tight places riddled with snags. He would tell me that sometimes you need to risk your flies to snags to catch the big fish.

Next time you set the hook and realize you have encountered a snag, stop the urge to continually yank the hook. This will only lodge it more. Release tension, then try to position yourself and the rod tip above and upstream of the snag. Think about how the flies came into the snag and pull the flies out the opposite way. Try to have your rod tip close to the water so if the flies do release, the extra length of leader does not shoot the flies high into the air and hook into overhead trees.

Before you even step into the water, take a moment to thoroughly stretch out the leader and fly line. Remove around 30 feet of leader and fly line from the reel. Gently stretch out the leader from the sighter material through to the fly line. The leader and fly line can become heavily coiled the longer the reel sits. Taking the time to stretch out the leader helps with accuracy, bite detection, and reducing tangles.

Strategy is important when attacking a new stream, or in this case during the world championship. Head coach Kalvin Kayloz, Martin Dietz, and Ben Comfort are planning a strategy for the US Youth team for their session in the Czech Republic. JOSH MILLER

7

Approach

Now that we have brought it all together, we need to strategize our approach. Have a plan of attack before approaching any section of water. Spots where fish are located in the water can change often, sometimes a few times a day. Fish go where the food is being offered. Usually, they go to the easiest and safest place that has available food. Fish move to different spots for cover and safety. Feeding spots change depending on water depth, temperature, and bug activity. So having a plan of attack is necessary to cover all places where a fish could be lurking.

For me, having a plan starts even before my first cast of the day, when I observe the water. I will not attach flies to my setup until I take a moment to assess the situation. I look to see if there are bugs flying around on the surface. If possible, I will try to visually spot fish and observe the way they react to passing food. This is a fun time to flip over a couple rocks to see what common bugs are active. You can then feel confident in picking a fly that matches size, profile, and color. Observation is important in forming a plan of approach.

If you witnessed fish eating or flashing, you now have a target and starting point. If there is no fish activity observed, then you can fall back to your backup or original plan. My backup approach while euro nymphing usually starts with the flies and drift that I am most confident with. I fish a medium-angled drift with a Walt's Worm and France Fly on a light leader. If that does not work, I have a sequence for the next fly, setup, and water type.

A section of river that looked like this is where I would confidently start when fishing a new place—especially if the stream was filled with wild trout and the water was in the 50s to low 60s. I like to ask my clients: Would you rather fish a single hole with 25 fish, or 25 small holes with 1 single fish? I would rather fish 25 places giving me 25 first-time chances than one spot, potentially spooking the other 24 fish after I catch 1! JOSH MILLER

Pro Tip

If you are confident there is one or more fish to be caught in a certain location, figure out what you need to change to catch that fish. Many anglers make a few casts and move on without analyzing the specific characteristics of their presentation that they can change. When you make that change and you catch a fish, you will better recognize how your presentation needs to change the next time you confront a similar situation. —Devin Olsen

When fishing a new place, or when starting off the day, find a place in the water you are most comfortable with. The water I will first approach is the type I am most comfortable catching fish in. If the water temperature is warmer, between 55 and 62°F, I tend to look for water that is faster and hopefully broken up into pockets with rocks. Water with a broken surface helps camouflage fish to overhead prey. My favorite water depth to fish is between ankle and waist deep. If the water is colder, under 55 degrees, I start at a place that has slightly slower water, between knee and waist deep if possible. My goal is to capture a fish quickly. This gives me confidence that I am using the correct approach and fly pattern. When an angler asks me what to do when going to a new stream for the first time, I tell them: Identify the best-looking water, fish the fly you have the most confidence in, and try to catch just one fish to give yourself confidence. If that plan does not work, it is important to have a backup plan.

Strategy is everything while fly fishing. Devin Olsen planned his approach on this section of river as he practiced for the world championship in Tasmania in 2019. MICHAEL BRADLEY

Choosing where to fish can be overwhelming, especially on new and larger waters. Small streams can be easier to read, and it is more obvious where fish should be holding. Take that mindset and break down a larger waterway by picturing it as a small stream. Sean Crocker shared this advice during a fishing session on a wide river in Colorado. He told me to try not to get overwhelmed by all the water. Just pick a small spot and break it down as you would a small stream. That mindset has now evolved to trying to grid the water into sections. Gridding off the stream will help us cover more holding spots.

Along with the approach, it is also important to discuss how you enter and position yourself in the water, called body positioning. Determine what target area you plan to fish. Find the best route to get to that spot without spooking fish, and fish your way to that spot. Setting yourself up to get the best drift and spook fewer fish will only help your success.

GRID SYSTEM

Fish sit in various places that we often walk right past without knowing. While guiding, I often see experienced anglers challenged to find all the potential feeding spots at different times. Where I catch fish often surprises me. Identifying likely holding spots and feeding zones is part of what we call reading the water. Reading the water is such an important concept, which anglers will

I like to have a way to cover holding spots, especially during times of glare or in water that is limited in features. Gridding the water into small sections will help you cover more holding areas. SARAH MILLER

Fishing large water can be intimidating. Roch Miller breaks down the river into areas that he can get to and properly fish. He first casts in the water that's closest to the bank. JOSH MILLER

continue to develop over their lifetime. For me, the way I read the water slowly adapts as I capture fish in different streams throughout the world. Fish are living and sometimes unpredictable creatures.

For some anglers, figuring out where the trout are seems second nature. I am sometimes surprised when those anglers know where to cast and when to adjust. Yet for myself and many others, it can be a long road of success and failure to develop this instinct. Luckily, using the grid system makes it easier to cover water. This significantly helps anglers recognize potentially good water that could otherwise be overlooked.

Gridding off the water helps you make sure to cover every spot. You will start catching fish in places that might surprise you. The practice of gridding water helps anglers learn more about where the fish are and focus on finding the next fish. For example, fish might still be holding at the tail of a pool looking for remnants of last night's spinner fall, or they might slide up into skinny water during a hatch. I would not have learned these trends if I only fished water I was comfortable with. While guiding, my students will cast right into the obviously fishy-looking water. This approach will yield a quickly caught fish but could spook other fish. Fish that are holding in skinny water sometimes are more wary of any overhead movements, like anglers or predatory birds. Often fish located in the shallows on the banks of the stream are spooked easily, but willing to eat a fly.

I missed this fish on the first cast when I spotted it holding in skinny water. Instead of recasting, I watched the fish's behavior, as it was now moving around and unsettled. I waited and did not move until it settled back down. On my next cast the fish happily ate my fly. JOE CLARK

The way I like to grid off water is to simply break the water into lanes. Only focus on the water that is within a reasonable distance. Start in the water closest to you. The distance we are fishing is within about 20 feet, so focus on that water first. Euro nymphing is most effective as a close-range technique. As you grid the water, you might be surprised that you catch fish where you would not think. Fish seem to disperse on highly trafficked streams that get frequently fished by euro nymphing techniques. Learning to grid the water will help an angler catch more fish.

PATIENCE

When we miss a fish, our natural inclination is to immediately cast back. Resting a fish takes patience and discipline. After you miss a fish, it will often reject your flies if you immediately cast back. A single minute is sometimes all it takes for a fish to reset. Hopefully in that time the fish has a chance to settle down, eat a few natural bugs, and accept your fly as it drifts past again.

The idea of resting a fish became a big part of my overall approach when competing. It took discipline to not cast directly back. I would stand still and take a moment to reflect, and focus, on the missed fish and the whole scenario. Use the concept we talked about earlier in this book, called learning from a drift. Then take some deep breaths, say a little prayer, and relax.

I may cast in another location while giving the fish a moment to settle and reset. I try to picture in my mind the fish returning to its feeding spot and eating a few bugs. Before you cast, zero into the exact location where the fish ate during the drift. As I cast, I am recoiled and ready to strike.

This mindset has helped me tremendously while competing on the national level. Every fish caught is important while competing, and a missed fish is one that gave up its location. Casting immediately back at a fish has a much lower success rate than giving the fish even 10 seconds to rest. It is surprising how many times a fish will eat again after a short rest. Try this trick next time you are out on the water and miss a fish!

LESSONS LEARNED

The following story is about how I progressed through my default technique to catch one of my largest trout to date. After spotting a giant fish, I worked through my approach, technique, and flies to entice it to eat. The main point of the story is patience, but there are many more lessons to learn, too.

While on a trip out West with my father, we were fishing in heavy pocket-water on a small mountain creek. The banks were lined with pine trees, and the sun was just breaking over the top of the mountain. The morning was cool with little wind. Fishing was good, and I was euro nymphing a pair of nymphs in the heavy water. Each little slot would provide me with an opportunity to catch a wild brown trout.

I came across the first longer pool in the stream. The sun's rays cutting through the pines revealed what looked like a gigantic fish holding in the lower

Stay in the shadows and move easily when approaching fish or a target spot. RODGER OBLEY

I use these rocks as a natural barrier to help mask my approach. If possible, I stand outside of the target area. DOMINIC LENTINI

end of the pool. The fish had bright pink sides and appeared to be a rainbow trout. My heart started pounding after I realized how big the fish was. I took a moment on the bank to settle down. I told myself, "Think, do not just cast . . . calm down, slow down your heart rate, and slow down your game plan." I took the time to switch to a slightly heavier leader, sighter, and tippet, and I switched from two flies down to only one.

I moved into a position close enough to visually see the fish. I wanted to observe how it might react to my flies as they drifted past. The stream contained many boulders and substrate creating various seams and disturbances. This gave me enough cover to know I could get close. The rocks and structure helped dampen the sound as I moved very slowly, without bumping rocks with my feet, into position. I was close enough that I could see the white flash of the trout's mouth as it ate a few passing bugs. I was positioned about 15 feet behind the fish, using a large rock as cover.

My first cast was with my confidence fly, a Walt's Worm. Making sure that the first cast was accurate, I knew I needed the fly to drift directly into the face of the resting fish. If the cast were off target or not going to drift in the right area, I would not allow the flies to touch the water. What I did not want to happen was for the flies to go more than a foot or two on either side of the fish. This could create a chance that the fish would turn after the passing flies, making it easy for the fish to spot me downstream. Sometimes when a big fish moves from its holding spot, it will become uncomfortable and spook easily. The cast was good, and the flies drifted right into the fish. I could see the fish move a little. The small movement the fish made was enough to tell me the fish was slightly active and might eat.

I learned a lot of fish body language while fishing for muskie with my friend Tim Zietek. When a muskie is following a streamer, sometimes it eats the fly or sometimes it just follows the fly all the way back to the boat. He told me that when a muskie is really interested while following the fly, the fish will shake and quiver its fins. I did not understand exactly what he was saying until I had a muskie follow my flies a few weeks later. The massive fish was right behind my fly coming quickly to the boat. I could see the fins and how tense the fish was overall, its body language telling me that it wanted to eat the fly. It did, and, of course, I muffed the hook set. The body language of a big trout can be like a muskie. The big fish showed interest in a different way, however, with a slight wave of its tail as the Walt's drifted by.

My natural impulse was to immediately cast the flies back at the fish; instead, I settled back down to think through my next move. I decided my next adjustment would be to change the fly to another confidence pattern, a Frenchie. The time it took me to pause, pray, think, and change the fly was a few minutes giving the fish time to calm, reset, and hopefully eat a few natural bugs.

Joe Humphreys uses the tuck cast to get his egg fly into a holding spot. Joe fished with intention and precision as he picked apart small areas of this stream. GORDON VANDERPOOL

Even with an accurate cast, the fish had no interest in the drifting Frenchie. It showed no movement or any other interest. I removed the fly and sat there thinking about what I should do. I tried to recall past experiences and similar situations. Thinking it was a rainbow trout, I decided my next fly would be an attractor.

I went to my working box and grabbed a small white egg. I remember having a similar experience while fishing with Joe Humphreys on the Blue River in Breckenridge, Colorado. We were fishing in a beautiful section of water just below a road bridge. Joe showed me how he would work the water with a nymph while catching a few small wild fish. He said there had to be a larger fish lurking in the depths of the hole. He grabbed his fly box and pulled out an egg pattern, which surprised me. But it only took a few casts and Joe brought a nice rainbow to hand.

I decided now was time to try that small, white egg fly. I cast, and the fish rose in the water column and got so close to the fly I swear it tried to smell it. The fish moved around a bit for a few seconds then quickly settled back down. My heart was racing, but I waited a moment to make the next cast. I thought the egg would do it on the next cast. But the fish just let the fly pass right by on the next drift.

Take a minute to observe the water before just jumping right in. Watch for any clues from nature like fish or bug activity. JOE CLARK

I was caught in tunnel vision and forgot to take a moment to view my surroundings. Nature will oftentimes give us hints to help us with the approach. I noticed some small black caddis bouncing around the water and in the pine trees. I yelled over to my pops, who had been standing on the bank witnessing the whole situation. He shook a tree, and when he did, loads of caddis flew out.

At this point, luckily, the sun was not totally shining on the water. There were still some shadows cutting through the trees, making it harder to see the fish. I grabbed a dark-colored Walt's Worm with a bright silver bead. I made the cast count by not letting the fly hit the water until I was happy with its position. The fly came in front of the fish, and it seemed super interested in it. Fins were moving and the fish began swimming around, appearing to be looking for the fly. Up until this point I had only made five casts in over 15 minutes of fishing. I did not want to blow up the fish by casting too many times and risking it spooking. Sometimes even the splash of the flies hitting the water over and over can easily spook a wary fish.

Going even deeper into my backup plan, I thought about what I should do next to change the drift. Caddis will swim actively to the surface, so on the next cast I tried to give the fly movement. As the fly sank to depth with little wrist movement, I gave the fly motion by jigging the rod tip quickly and abruptly, moving the flies up and down. The jigging motion was accompanied by a second of pause so the flies would sink back to depth. The fish noticed the movement and quickly ate the jigged Walt's. I finally got it. There are many lessons to learn even while fishing for one fish. Take the time to learn, notice visual cues, slow down, and always have a plan.

BODY POSITION

Catching fish can depend on getting your body into the right position on the stream. Euro nymphing is a close-range technique. Getting yourself into the best spot to make good drifts is important. It takes time to learn how close we can get to the fish without spooking them.

I try to get positioned close enough to fish so the best part of my drift is in the target zone. A likely fish holding area can sometimes be ridiculously small, such as tiny pockets or broken water with narrow seams. Getting a close position is crucial for an accurate cast and proper drift into these areas. Good body position is also necessary to help keep the flies at a target place for longer amounts of time. If we try to fish from too far away, extra tension could create drag and cause the flies to swim unnaturally, spooking fish on the first drift.

The closer you are, the better control you will have over the flies. A closer position helps manage tension and minimize drag. Fishing close to the rod tip will also help control the drift better. Being close will improve your reaction time from when you see a strike to setting the hook. In addition, sometimes

When moving into position, I try to pick my lane wisely. Here I use underwater rocks and structure to hide my approach while targeting fish on a spring creek. JOE CLARK

we need to suspend our flies from the stream bottom. Fishing closer under the rod tip allows us to suspend the flies with control.

There is a balance between fishing at a distance and getting *too* close, spooking fish. Every stream is different, and how close you can get changes often. Here are some simple rules I use when approaching a spot. Knowing the target fish, how they react, and how spooky they are will help you decide what distance to position yourself. Water type and speed are the first important factors for knowing how close you can get. The more broken and quicker the water is, the

Pro Tip

Always try to keep your shadow off the water. Nothing spooks shallow trout like the sudden shadow of a predator. —Pat Weiss

closer you can get. Broken water is noisy, and the disturbance on the surface will help disguise anglers.

Water that is slower with more uniform currents is more difficult to fish. It is easier for the fish to see and feel us as we move into position. Water that is around waist deep can be more challenging to fish, especially when there are limited rocks and structure to break the sound of an approaching angler. These situations might limit how close we can get without spooking too many fish. Fishing over a greater distance might be necessary.

If I walk upstream to the next spot and spook a fish, it can become a chain reaction. That fish then takes off upstream just to spook the next fish in line all the way to the head of the pool. Knowing the fish and how they react will help you decide how close you can get. Sometimes you can get super close and the fish do not seem to care. One way to ascertain the situation is by slowly approaching and observing how close you can get until fish spook.

Water clarity is the next factor I consider when determining my position and distance. I love it when I arrive at a stream and see a deep green color. That color is a trademark of our Pennsylvania limestone streams. A good rule to start with is that the more color the water has, the closer I can position to my drift. A bright, sunny day can also affect how spooky the trout might be.

After determining the target area, get close and angle your toes into the current. This will turn your shoulder, positioning you to fish at an upstream

After moving into the target position, take a moment and be still. Fish will hopefully resume eating as you stand there and be easier to catch. Here I fish on my knees, or you can try to use low spots in the stream to keep a low profile to the fish. DOMINIC LENTINI

I spotted this fish sitting in shallow pocketwater on the edge of the river. I took a moment to observe my surroundings and produce a plan of approach. From past experience, I knew I could get close without spooking this fish. Getting close would help me get a good drift, increasing my chances to identify a bite, react, and land the fish. ROCH MILLER

Torrey Collins uses this large rock as cover as he sneaks up to a large fish in this run. He also positions his body upstream by facing his toes into the current. JOSH MILLER

angle. An upstream cast will help slow down a drift. This is because an upstream cast will fish closer to the water underneath the rod tip. The opposite would be to cast across the stream, where there are more current lanes and speeds. An upstream drift will spook fewer fish because our body position is behind the fish. The ideal body position is slightly downstream of the target.

During guide days I often see anglers square up to the water to fish directly across from their position. This approach may work sometimes, but it will spook more fish. The trick is to approach fish from behind and cast to them from downstream. Fish have a broad range of vision, but their sight is limited from behind. I will often remind anglers over the course of a day to turn their body position quartered upstream.

Another important part of an upstream drift is the hook set. Anytime we cast and drift to fish upstream (Zone A), we have a much greater chance of a clean hook set and landing that fish. When we get takes from fish downstream of our position (Zone B), we have a greater chance of a miss. The reason is, while drifting upstream we will be connecting to the fish with a downstream hook set. The fly will be coming backward into the mouth of the trout as opposed to setting the hook upstream and potentially stealing the lunch from the fish's mouth.

HOLD OR FOLD

Adjustments are one of the biggest variables in fly fishing. How do I know when it is time to move to another spot, change my technique, or switch flies? These are open-ended questions that take more than a few paragraphs to answer. Following are some examples and rules that I use that help me know when to move or adjust.

Many times I see anglers camped out fishing one spot for a long time. Many anglers get stuck and will not move much at all. Even just moving in small increments while fishing might be all it takes to catch more fish. I moved just a single step and immediately caught another fish. Another method is to fish quickly, covering substantial amounts of water.

Anglers who move quickly up the stream seem to catch more fish—at first. I liked this approach when I first started. I would quickly move from the top of one run to the next, only fishing the best-looking spots. Consequently, I would catch the easy fish that were willing to eat from the best parts of the runs. This was a good learning lesson to practice using simple techniques through repetitive success. The problem is that anglers might be passing up many other fish just to catch the eager ones. When fishing gets harder, anglers might struggle even more with this approach. Fishing the more challenging water will help you improve your technique and instinct.

If you are targeting larger fish, sometimes covering more water by moving quickly is the best method. I have seen the apex brown trout that sit in the best

Sometimes a single weight change is all it takes to catch a fish on the next drift. This brown trout was sitting next to the bank in a series of pocketwater. I only needed to change from a 2.8 mm to a 3.2 mm Walt's to catch this fish on the next drift. ROCH MILLER

Pro Tip

If you are more interested in larger fish than numbers, fish the prime lies at the head of the run with larger food items first. Otherwise the biggest active fish are likely to be spooked by the smaller fish you hook fishing up through the run. —Joe Goodspeed

water at the top of a run. Quickly moving from each place to fish the best water could be the way to target bigger fish.

In the cold months, a good approach is to move more consistently while covering slower water. I call this approach my winter technique. I use the grid method described earlier in this chapter and quickly cast to each section until I get a bite. Once I get a take or catch a fish, I then plant roots and fish that spot much more slowly. Fish sit together in pods in the winter. Find the pod using the grid method and prospect with an attractor. Once you find fish, slow down your approach.

When you have found the fish, moving a few inches will help show the flies at different speeds and depths. Anglers can drift the same area after moving (which may have been a stretch a few inches before), allowing the flies to slow down even more. Flies will drift through that run differently each time an angler moves. The start of a drift begins when the flies first touch the water, and we should be in a ready position for a potential strike. At times, the fish want it very slow; usually this is the middle of the drift. Lastly, there are times they want flies as they rise from the bottom. This take usually occurs at the end of each drift. Moving after a few casts will help the same fish see the flies come by in different ways.

Consistency in moving will also help you cover more fish. When anglers ask me how to catch more fish, I may respond with the basic concept of casting over more fish. Increased movement using the grid will yield a greater number of fish. Sometimes on guided trips we may take a step with every cast. I ask my students to move so many times during the day, but by the end of the session we may have only moved 100 yards. The movements we are making are not measured in feet but in inches.

Moving only a few inches in any direction will give us a different angle on the target spots. Euro nymphing in general is a close-distance technique, between 10 and 30 feet. There are parts of the drift that are better or present the fly in a different way. If we chop up a single drift, we can see that each part yields a different presentation of our flies. At the beginning of the drift the flies sink. At the middle part of the drift, we should be well connected with a

The Vltava River during the Youth World Championship had endless amounts of pockets and micro seams. To cover that much water can take a lot of an angler's time. The key to this river on that day was to make one or two casts in each spot that would result in a fish, a miss, or no bite. The fish would eat the fly on the first or second cast. Any extra casts were a waste of time. The tempo was to get into position, make a good cast or two, and move on, covering the most holding spots possible to maximize the catch. JOSH MILLER

slower speed. Toward the end of the drift, our flies will begin to rise toward the surface.

FIRST CAST

The first cast is crucial. It is the best chance to get the fish to eat that fly. Each drift after the fish has seen the fly decreases your chances. If you miss a fish, do not just immediately cast directly back at that fish (we are all guilty of this). Wait

a moment, relax, and give the fish a moment to regroup.

When approaching a new spot, run, pocket, or any new water, the first cast is a fresh new chance to cast over a new fish that has not seen your flies yet. The best way to maximize each new spot is to make the first cast count. Making the cast count means taking a moment to read the water and placing the flies in the target spot with accuracy and intention. Observe the water and figure out the target. Accuracy is a must with casting. I teach anglers the following steps: Get into position, place an accurate cast, limit backcasting to one, and make the first drift count.

The first cast in a new spot is the best chance to catch a fish. Sometimes the first cast is your only chance. This fish ate a well-placed Walt's Worm on the first cast. ROCH MILLER

Knowing where to cast takes time and practice. Conditions can dictate how many fish can be caught from one area. On the first cast, hooking one fish could spook the rest of the fish in that area. In this situation, casting to the top of the run and letting the flies pass all the fish could be your best chance. The opposite would be the case if the fish are not as spooky or are hungry. Just know that the first cast is our best chance, and we should make that our best drift—be ready to set the hook!

HAPPY FEET

When you hook a fish, assess the situation. Anglers can get so excited when they hook a fish. We call this "happy feet." Plant your feet and try to control

I love to catch big fish; who doesn't? I have seen too many fish lost when anglers panic. Next time you hook the big one, assess what is going on. Look around and identify obstacles the fish might try to run to. Identify a good and safe place to land the fish. Take your time!
SARAH MILLER

Stay cool and calm after hooking your next fish. RODGER OBLEY

the fish without moving, if possible. Next time you hook a fish, do nothing for 10 seconds. Assess the situation. Ten seconds are enough time to allow the fish to realize it is hooked and do a quick run. It also gives you a moment to gather your thoughts and figure out if the fish is big or not, and gives you enough time to observe your surroundings to locate a good place to land and fight the fish.

My goal as an angler and instructor is to encourage deeper thinking, more analyzation, and the willingness to adjust. Fly fishing at a high level is understanding what technique and approach to use at start, when to switch, and how to adjust. The flexibility of Euro nymphing a good piece of the fly-fishing puzzle. Never stop learning.

INDEX

anchor flies, 61, 120
approach. *See* strategy and approach
Armstrong, Jerry, xxv, *xxv*
attractor flies, 67–68, *68*

bead color: for fast water and whitewater, 71; fly pattern and, 68–72, *69*, *71*; rainbow trout and, 69, 70, 71, *71*, 72; weather and, 68
Bear, Roe, 31–32
beat, xviii–xix
bite detection: adjustments around, 96, 101–3; cold weather and, 97, *97*; concentration on, xvi, 97, 98, *98*, 101–2; euro nymphing opportunities for, 97; fly weight and, 60, 111; lightweight leader and, 44; polarized sunglasses and, 29; sag and, 100, 117, 132; seeing and counting missed bites and, xv–xvi, 2, 97; by sight and feel, xv, 1, 96; sighter role in, 1–2, 96; subtlety of, 58–59; tippet length and false, 123
blood knot, 19, 47–48, 50, 61
body position and posture, 86; arm close and low in, 11, *11*; arm extension and, 9–10; control of, 104–5; drifts and, 145; hiding approach with, 145–46, *146*; on knees, 147, *147*; large fish and, 148, *148*; shadow awareness and, 146; spooking fish considerations in, *146*, 146–47, 148; upstream angle and, 147, 149; water conditions and types relation to, 146–47; when hooking a fish, 154–55, *155*. *See also* casting
Bone, Drew, 102, *102*

Bosnia, *xxi*
Bourcq, Paul, 108, 115
Bower, David, *3*
Bradley, Michael, *12*
Bread-n-Butter Nymph (fly pattern), 77, *77*
brown trout, xviii, *xviii*, *114*; bead color and, 70; behavior, 115; fly profile and, 64; fly weight change for catching, 150, *150*; net size for large, 33, *33*
bugs, 26, *26*; jigging flies technique mimicking, 130; observation of, 130, *144*, 144–45; single-fly setup and fish preference of, 53
Burgdorff, Cody, 45, 46

Cammisa, Tim, 77
carryall, 35, *35*
casting: accuracy, 82, *82*, 83, 87, 153; adjustments with different water conditions, 80, *80–81*; bouncing sighter after, 13; bow and arrow, 5, *5*, 90–91, *91*; control of, 104; drifts and drift speed and, 87, 128, 149; euro compared with traditional, 81; in fast water and whitewater, 126; finding sighter after, 98–99; first cast importance in, 152–54, *153*; flick technique, 86–87; Frisbee, 44, 83, 84–87, *85*, 116, 126; getting flies deeper with, 111–12; leader length and, 81; mix of overhead with low-angle, 83; movement between, 151–52; 180 rule, 44, 83–84, 85, 86; overhead, alternatives to, 5, *5*; paint strokes kinship with, 3; patience and, 87,

goal of, 95; hook set and position of, 100, 101; hook set and upstream, 149; knowing variety of techniques for, 94; leader length and control of, 38; leader weight for control of, 44, *44*; lead the flies technique and, 125–28, *126–27*; learning from, 101–3, *102*; longer rods for controlling, 8, 9; multiple-fly setup and, 49, 52, *52–53*, 61; one hand trick for close range control of, *121*, 121–22; paint strokes kinship with, 3; rod angle for control of, xiv, *xiv–xv*, xxiv, 3, *3*, 95, *95*, 104, 105, 106, *106–7*, 109, *109*, 110; rod movements and, 104–5; sequence and position, *99*, 99–103, 151–52; sighter for gauging, 96; slow/slowing down, xiv, *xiv–xv*, xxii, xxiv, *3*, 28, 95, *95*, 109–10, 118, *118*, 128, 149; SMD technique for controlling, 114–18, *117*, *118*; spooking fish with sloppy, 99; thinner tippet for slowing, 28; tippet length and, 113, 118; understanding, xx, 93–99, 113; weather and fish response to, 95–96
dry-fly fishing: euro rods for, 8, 15, 16; jigging flies and, 130; leaders, 40; limited opportunities with, 4

Egan, Lance, 75, 76
eggs, 22
euro nymphing: about, xx–xxi, xxii, *xxvi*, 1–4; bite detection opportunities with, 97; gear differences in, 1, 2; transitioning from traditional nymph to, 17. *See also specific topics*

family, *xxiii*
fast water and whitewater, 72, 101, 103; bead color and, 71; casting in, 126; fishing success in, xxi–xxii, 6, *6*, 57; fly considerations in, 61, 63, *63*, 71, 110, 111, 126; hiding approach of angler, 146–47; net size and, 33, *33*; vector line management in, 108

fish behavior, 94, 115; attractor flies and, 67–68, *68*; drifts and, 95–96, 99–103; food detection and, 3; large bodies of water, 53; large flies and, 64; muskie, 143; observation of, xvi, 135, 140, *140*, 143, 144, *144*; subsurface feeding percentage and, 4; trout body language and, xvi, 3, 4, 115, 143; weather-related, 95–96, 97, *97*. *See also* spooking fish
fishing packs, 28
fish safety: hooks for, 72; tippets and, 112
flies: anchor, 61, 120; for competitions, 23, 26, 57–58; for dirty or cloudy water, 22; dropper, attachment of, 48–49; euro and traditional, compared, 56; for fast water and whitewater, 61, 63, *63*, 71, 110, 111, 126; jigging, 16, *129*, 129–30; leaders for large and bulky, 43; "oh crap," for challenging conditions, 22; practicing with and learning from different, 22, 72; rod design for bulkier, 13; simplicity and limiting selection of, xxiv, 25, 26, 55–56, 57–58; size ranges, 57; snags, 132–33, *133*; split shot and, xxii, 4, 58, 60, 111; tying, benefits of, 61, 62; water loading and, 81, 83, 87; working box for, xxii, 22, *23*, *24*, 25–26, 27, *27*. *See also* bead color; drifts and drift speed; hooks; sink rate
flies, connection with, 26; floating the sighter and, 122–23; fly weight and, 62; importance of, 58–59; lead the flies technique for, 125–27, *126–27*; lightweight leaders for, 36, *36*, 44; longer rods aiding, 9; sighter role in, 98; single-fly setup and, 53; split shot and, 58
floating the sighter technique, xxv, 42, *125*; about, 94; current and sighter control in, 122–23, *123*; in deeper water, 123; drift position and, 100; fly line for, 19; goal and benefits of, 122,

fly weight and, 111; lead the flies technique for turbulent, 125–26, *126–27*; learning variety of techniques for, 117; single-fly setup for varied, 52, *52*; testing out techniques in different, 92. *See also* deep water; dirty or cloudy water; fast water and whitewater; shallow, medium, and deep technique; shallow water

water grid technique, xxii, xxiv, *138*, 138–40, *139*

wax, 30; for floating the sighter technique, 125; sighter wax, 31–33, *32*

weather, 20; bead color and, 68; fish behavior related to, 95–96, 97, *97*. *See also* cold weather; low-light conditions; wind

Weigand, Tess, *2*, *32*

weighted flies. *See* fly weight

Weiss, Pat, *xvii*, xix, 37, 64; fly pattern designs, *77*; techniques, xvii, 31, *31*, 48, 125, *125*, 146

Weiss' Simple PTN (fly pattern), 77, *77*

Westbrook, Jess, 76

wet-fly fishing rods, 15

whitewater. *See* fast water and whitewater

Williams, Loren, xix

wind: casting techniques in, 16, 83, 86; fly line weight for, 19; Frisbee cast and, 86; leader adjustments for, 38, 39, 40, 41

World Fly Fishing Championship, 44

Yardley, Nick, 119, *119*

Young, Walt, 74

Youth Team. *See* US Youth Fly Fishing Team

Zone Stone (fly pattern), 75, *75*

ABOUT THE AUTHOR

Josh Miller was a member of the 2016–2020 Fly Fishing Team USA. He led the US youth team to a gold medal in the 2023 World Championship in Bosnia and Herzegovina. He has competed in the regional and national competition circuits as well as assistant-coached in three World Youth Fly Fishing Championships. Miller is a full-time guide and traveling instructor, and also a signature tier for companies such as Orvis and Fulling Mill. Miller endorses Thomas & Thomas rods and scientific anglers and lives with his wife, Sarah, and his son, Jonah, in western Pennsylvania.